family circle®

Deli food to make at home

The Family Circle® Promise of Success

Welcome to the world of Confident Cooking,
created for you in the Australian **Family Circle**®
Test Kitchen, where recipes are double-tested by
our team of home economists to achieve a
high standard of success—and delicious
results every time.

M U R D O C H   B O O K S®
Sydney • London • Vancouver • New York

C O N T E

Marinated chilli mushrooms, page 9

Smoked salmon tartlets, page 25

Marinated feta, page 64

Pizza-topped focaccia, page 85

N T S

Pear and almond flan, page 99

Baklava, page 109

The Publisher thanks the following for their assistance. Hale Imports, Country Floors, Empire Homewares, Pillivuyt, Chief Australia, Sunbeam Corporation Ltd, Kambrook, Sheldon & Hammond, Bertoli Olive Oil; Southcorp Appliances. **Front cover:** Spinach and feta triangles (page 34). **Inside front cover:** Marinated bocconcini (page 86).

All recipes are double-tested by our team of home economists. When we test our recipes, we rate them for ease of preparation. The following cookery ratings are on the recipes in this book, making them easy to use and understand.

A single Cooking with Confidence symbol indicates a recipe that is simple and generally quick to make —perfect for beginners.

Two symbols indicate the need for just a little more care and a little more time.

Three symbols indicate special dishes that need more investment in time, care and patience—but the results are worth it.

IMPORTANT

Those who might be at risk from the effects of salmonella food poisoning (the elderly, pregnant women, young children and those suffering from immune deficiency diseases) should consult their GP with any concerns about eating raw eggs.

Chocolate and hazelnut friands, page 90

Passionfruit melting moments, page 94

MEDITERRANEAN LAYERED COB

Preparation time: 45 minutes +
  30 minutes standing + overnight
  refrigeration
Total cooking time: 30 minutes
Serves 6

2 eggplants
4 zucchini
900 g (1³/4 lb) orange sweet
  potato
2 large red capsicums
1/3 cup (80 ml/2³/4 fl oz) olive oil
23 cm (9 inch) round cob loaf
165 g (5¹/2 oz) jar pesto
200 g (6¹/2 oz) ricotta cheese
1/3 cup (35 g/1¹/4 oz) grated
  Parmesan

1 Cut the eggplants and zucchini into 1 cm (¹/2 inch) slices lengthways. Set the zucchini aside and put the eggplant slices in a colander. Sprinkle with salt and leave for 30 minutes, then rinse well and pat dry with paper towels.
2 Cut the sweet potato into 5 mm (¹/4 inch) slices. Quarter the capsicums and remove the seeds and membranes.

Grill, skin-side-up, until the skins have blistered and blackened. Place in a plastic bag, leave to cool, then remove the skins. Brush the eggplant, sweet potato and zucchini with olive oil and chargrill, grill or barbecue in batches until lightly browned.
3 Cut the lid from the top of the loaf. Remove the soft bread from inside the loaf, leaving a 1 cm (¹/2 inch) shell. Brush the inside of the loaf and lid with the pesto. Layer the zucchini and capsicum inside the loaf, then spread with the combined ricotta and Parmesan. Layer the sweet potato and eggplant inside the loaf, lightly pressing down to fit. Replace the lid.
4 Cover the loaf with plastic wrap and place on a baking tray. Place another tray on top of the loaf and put heavy weights or food cans on top of the tray. Refrigerate overnight.
5 Preheat the oven to very hot 250°C (500°F/Gas 10). Remove the plastic wrap, return the loaf to the baking tray and bake for about 10 minutes, or until crispy. Cut into wedges to serve.

NUTRITION PER SERVE
Protein 13 g; Fat 20 g; Carbohydrate 37 g; Dietary Fibre 6 g; Cholesterol 22 mg; 1565 kJ (373 cal)

Use a sharp knife to cut the sweet potato into 5 mm (¹/4 inch) slices.

Remove the soft bread inside the loaf with a metal spoon.

Layer the eggplant and sweet potato inside the loaf, pressing down to fit.

Put another tray over the loaf, and top with heavy weights or food cans.

HERB BAKED RICOTTA

Preparation time: 25 minutes +
overnight refrigeration
Total cooking time: 30 minutes
Serves 4

1 kg (2 lb) wedge full-fat ricotta
(see Note)
2 tablespoons fresh thyme
leaves
2 tablespoons chopped fresh
rosemary
2 tablespoons chopped fresh
oregano

1/4 cup (15 g/1/2 oz) chopped
fresh parsley
1/4 cup (15 g/1/2 oz) chopped
fresh chives
2 cloves garlic, crushed
1/2 cup (125 ml/4 fl oz) olive oil

1 Pat the ricotta dry with paper towels
and place in a baking dish.
2 Mix together the herbs, garlic, oil
and 2 teaspoons of cracked pepper in
a bowl. Spoon the herb mixture onto
the ricotta, pressing with the back of a
metal spoon to make the herbs stick.
Cover and refrigerate overnight.
3 Preheat the oven to moderate 180°C

(350°F/Gas 4). Bake for 30 minutes,
or until the ricotta is set. Delicious
served with crusty bread.

NUTRITION PER SERVE
Protein 25 g; Fat 60 g; Carbohydrate 3 g;
Dietary Fibre 0 g; Cholesterol 120 mg;
2707 kJ (645 cal)

COOK'S FILE

Note: If you can't buy a wedge of
ricotta, put the ricotta pieces in a
colander and drain overnight in a
large bowl. Spread half the herb
mixture in a 1.25 litre loaf tin; spoon
the ricotta in and spread with the
remaining herbs before baking.

*Using a sharp knife, chop the rosemary,
oregano, parsley and chives.*

*Add 2 teaspoons of cracked black pepper
to the herbs and garlic.*

*Press the herb mixture onto the ricotta
with the back of a metal spoon.*

Stir the frothy yeast and oil into the flour and salt until well combined.

Flatten one portion of dough into a rectangle and put the basil and garlic on top.

Punch down the dough with your fist to expel the air.

Divide the dough into 12 portions and roll into sticks.

GRISSINI

Preparation time: 30 minutes +
1 hour 10 minutes standing
Total cooking time: 20 minutes
Makes 24

7 g (¹/₄ oz) sachet dried yeast
1 teaspoon sugar
4 cups (500 g/1 lb) plain flour
¹/₄ cup (60 ml/2 fl oz) olive oil
¹/₄ cup (15 g/¹/₂ oz) chopped
   fresh basil
4 cloves garlic, crushed
¹/₂ cup (50 g/1³/₄ oz) finely
   grated Parmesan
2 teaspoons sea salt flakes
2 tablespoons finely grated
   Parmesan, extra

1 Combine the yeast, sugar and 1¹/₄ cups (315 ml/10 fl oz) warm water in a small bowl and leave in a warm place for about 5–10 minutes, or until frothy. Sift the flour and 1 teaspoon salt into a bowl and stir in the frothy yeast and oil until the mixture is combined. Add more water if the dough is dry.
2 Gather the dough into a ball and turn out onto a lightly floured surface. Knead for 10 minutes, or until soft

and elastic. Divide the dough into two portions, add the basil and garlic to one portion, and the Parmesan to the other. The best way to do this is to flatten the dough into a rectangle and place the filling on top. Fold the dough to enclose the filling, then knead for a few minutes to incorporate evenly.
3 Place the doughs into two lightly oiled bowls and cover with plastic wrap. Leave in a warm place for about 1 hour, or until doubled in volume. Preheat the oven to very hot 230°C (450°F/Gas 8) and lightly grease two large baking trays.
4 Punch down the doughs and knead each again for 1 minute. Divide the two pieces of dough into 12 portions each, and roll each portion into a stick about 30 cm (12 inches) long and 5 mm (¹/₄ inch) across. Place on the baking trays and brush with some water. Sprinkle the basil and garlic dough with the sea salt flakes, and the cheese dough with the extra Parmesan. Bake for 15 minutes, or until crisp and golden brown.

NUTRITION PER GRISSINI
Protein 3.5 g; Fat 3.5 g; Carbohydrate 16 g; Dietary Fibre 1 g; Cholesterol 3 mg; 457 kJ (109 cal)

COOK'S FILE

Storage time: Grissini will keep stored in an airtight container for up to 1 week.

PRESERVED LEMONS

Preparation time: 20 minutes +
　6 weeks standing
Total cooking time: Nil
Fills a 1-litre jar

**6 thin-skinned lemons
　(see Note)
100 g (3¹/₂ oz) salt
2 cups (500 ml/16 fl oz)
　lemon juice**

1 Wash and scrub the lemons well in warm water to remove any wax. Slice off the stems, then cut each lemon in half lengthways. Cut each half in half again without cutting all the way through, leaving the two pieces attached. Sprinkle some of the salt generously over each cut portion; then pack some more salt between the cut portions.
2 Rinse a wide-necked, clip-top, 1-litre jar with boiling water and dry in a warm oven (do not dry with a tea towel). Pack the lemons into the jar tightly and add the remaining salt. (The tighter you pack the jar, the less lemon juice you will use, and the fewer air gaps there will be, giving a better result.)
3 Pour the lemon juice into the jar until the lemons are covered. (It may not be necessary to use all the lemon juice.) Seal and gently turn the jar over to dissolve the salt. Leave in a cool, dark place for 6 weeks. Turn the jar over daily for the first 2 weeks.
4 Once opened, store the lemons in the refrigerator. To use, rinse with water to remove any excess salt and discard the flesh. Only the rind is used, which can be sliced or chopped and used in a variety of dishes. Alternatively, try stirring the lemons into a Moroccan-style couscous.

Nutritional analysis is not appropriate for this recipe.

COOK'S FILE

Note: For best results, check with your fruit and vegetable market for a variety of thin-skinned lemon, such as Meyer.
Variation: Try adding a cinnamon stick, cloves and a bay leaf to the jar with the lemons.

Scrub the lemons thoroughly in warm water to remove any wax.

Cut each lemon half in half again, taking care not to cut all the way through.

Pack a generous amount of salt in-between the cut lemon portions.

Pour lemon juice into the jar until the lemons are fully covered.

MARINATED CHILLI MUSHROOMS

Preparation time: 20 minutes +
  overnight refrigeration
Total cooking time: Nil
Serves 8 (as part of an antipasto platter)

750 g (1½ lb) button
  mushrooms
2 cups (500 ml/16 fl oz)
  light olive oil
2 tablespoons lemon juice
1 clove garlic, finely chopped
¼ teaspoon caster sugar
1 red chilli, finely chopped

1 green chilli, finely chopped
1 tablespoon chopped fresh
  coriander
1 tablespoon chopped fresh
  flat-leaf parsley

1 Wipe the mushrooms with a damp paper towel to remove any dirt and place in a bowl.
2 Mix together the oil, lemon juice, garlic, sugar and chilli. Pour over the mushrooms and mix well so that the mushrooms are evenly coated. Cover with plastic wrap and marinate in the refrigerator overnight.
3 Just before serving, add the herbs, season and mix well.

NUTRITION PER SERVE
Protein 3.5 g; Fat 1.5 g; Carbohydrate 2 g; Dietary Fibre 2.5 g; Cholesterol 0 mg; 150 kJ (35 cal)

COOK'S FILE

Note: The coriander and parsley are added just before serving to retain their colour. If you prefer a stronger flavour, add them before marinating.
Serving suggestion: Marinated mushrooms can be served as part of an antipasto platter, along with a selection of sun-dried vegetables, marinated artichokes, caperberries and toasted bruschetta, and whatever else you would like to serve.

Wipe the mushrooms with a damp paper towel to remove any dirt.

Pour the combined oil, lemon juice, garlic, sugar and chilli over the mushrooms.

Chop the coriander and parsley and add to the mushrooms just before serving.

SALMON PATTIES

Preparation time: 30 minutes +
  30 minutes refrigeration
Total cooking time: 40 minutes
Makes 8

3 potatoes, cut into pieces
30 g (1 oz) butter
1 onion, finely chopped
1 clove garlic, crushed
1 red capsicum, finely chopped
415 g (13¹/4 oz) can pink salmon
1 egg, lightly beaten
2 tablespoons lemon juice
¹/4 cup (15 g/¹/2 oz) chopped
  fresh parsley
3 tablespoons plain flour
1 egg, lightly beaten, extra
2 tablespoons milk
1 cup (100 g/3¹/2 oz) dry
  breadcrumbs
oil, for shallow-frying

1 Boil the potatoes until tender, drain and return to the pan. Stir over medium heat, then mash. Melt the butter in a frying pan, then fry the onion and garlic over medium heat for 5 minutes, or until soft. Add the capsicum and cook, stirring, for a further 5 minutes, or until soft.
2 Drain the salmon, remove any dark skin and bones and flake roughly with a fork in a bowl. Mix in the cooled potato, beaten egg, onion mixture, lemon juice and parsley. (The mixture should still have a few pieces of salmon in it and will be a little soft.)
3 Form the mixture into eight patties. Coat the patties in the flour, then in the combined egg and milk, and then in the breadcrumbs. Place on a plate or baking tray. Reshape if necessary, then cover and chill for 30 minutes.

4 Heat the oil in a heavy-based frying pan. Shallow-fry the patties in batches for 2–3 minutes on each side, or until golden brown. Drain and serve hot.

NUTRITION PER PATTY
Protein 15 g; Fat 11 g; Carbohydrate 19 g; Dietary Fibre 2 g; Cholesterol 95 mg; 1012 kJ (242 cal)

Using a fork, roughly flake the drained salmon into a bowl.

Coat the patties in the combined egg and milk, and then in the breadcrumbs.

Shallow-fry the patties in hot oil until golden brown on both sides.

TABBOULEH

Preparation time: 25 minutes +
  30 minutes refrigeration
Total cooking time: Nil
Serves 8

1 cup (175 g/6 oz) burghul
2 teaspoons olive oil
1 cup (30 g/1 oz) chopped fresh
  flat-leaf parsley
1 cup (50 g/1¾ oz) chopped
  fresh mint

¾ cup (90 g/3 oz) finely
  chopped spring onions
4 Roma tomatoes, chopped
½ cup (125 ml/4 fl oz) olive oil
½ cup (125 ml/4 fl oz) lemon
  juice
2 cloves garlic, crushed

1 Put the burghul in a bowl and pour in 1 cup (250 ml/8 fl oz) boiling water. Mix in the olive oil, then set aside for 10 minutes. Stir again and cool.
2 Add the herbs, spring onion and tomato to the burghul and mix well.

Whisk the oil, lemon juice and garlic together and add to the burghul. Mix gently and season well. Cover and chill for 30 minutes before serving.

NUTRITION PER SERVE
Protein 6 g; Fat 20 g; Carbohydrate 7.5 g; Dietary Fibre 5 g; Cholesterol 0 mg; 1028 kJ (245 cal)

COOK'S FILE

Variation: Burghul is also sold as bulgur or cracked wheat. If you prefer, couscous can be used instead of the burghul in this recipe.

Finely chop the Roma tomatoes with a sharp knife.

Pour the olive oil into the bowl of burghul and mix well.

Add the herbs, spring onion and tomato to the burghul.

BEEF AND RED WINE PIES

Preparation time: 50 minutes
Total cooking time: 2 hours 40 minutes
Makes 6

1/4 cup (60 ml/2 fl oz) oil
1 1/2 kg (3 lb) chuck steak, cubed
2 onions, chopped
1 clove garlic, crushed
1/4 cup (30 g/1 oz) plain flour
1 1/4 cups (315 ml/10 fl oz)
    good-quality dry red wine
2 cups (500 ml/16 fl oz)
    beef stock
2 bay leaves
2 sprigs fresh thyme
2 carrots, chopped
4 sheets ready-rolled shortcrust
    pastry
1 egg, lightly beaten
4 sheets ready-rolled puff
    pastry

1 Heat 2 tablespoons of the oil in a large pan, add the meat and fry in batches until browned all over. Heat the remaining oil in the same pan, add the onion and garlic and stir over medium heat until golden brown. Add the flour and stir over medium heat for 2 minutes, or until well browned.

2 Remove from the heat and gradually stir in the combined wine and stock. Return to the heat and stir until the mixture boils and thickens. Return the meat to the pan with the bay leaves and thyme, and simmer for 1 hour. Add the carrot and simmer for a further 45 minutes, or until the meat and carrot are tender and the sauce has thickened. Season to taste, and remove the bay leaves and thyme sprigs. Cool.

3 Preheat the oven to moderately hot 200°C (400°F/Gas 6). Lightly grease six metal pie tins measuring 9 cm (3 1/2 inches) along the base and 3 cm (1 1/4 inches) deep. Cut the shortcrust pastry sheets in half diagonally. Line the base and side of each pie tin with the pastry and trim the edges. Line each pie with baking paper and fill with baking beads. Place on a baking tray and bake for 8 minutes. Remove the paper and beads and bake for a further 8 minutes, or until the pastry is lightly browned. Cool.

4 Spoon the filling into the pastry cases and brush the edge with some of the beaten egg. Cut the puff pastry sheets in half diagonally and cover the tops of the pies. Trim the excess, pressing the edges with a fork to seal. Cut a slit in the top of each pie. Brush the tops with the remaining egg, and bake for 20–25 minutes, or until the pastry is golden brown.

NUTRITION PER PIE
Protein 60 g; Fat 47 g; Carbohydrate 51 g; Dietary Fibre 3.3 g; Cholesterol 200 mg; 3648 kJ (873 cal)

Fry the steak in batches in a large pan until browned all over.

Line the base and side of each pie tin with the shortcrust pastry.

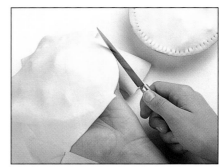

Cover the filling with puff pastry and trim off the excess.

CARAMELISED ONION AND POTATO SALAD

Preparation time: 20 minutes
Total cooking time: 1 hour
Serves 10

oil, for cooking
6 red onions, thinly sliced
1 kg (2 lb) Kipfler or new
    potatoes (see Note), unpeeled
4 rashers bacon, rind removed
2/3 cup (30 g/1 oz) fresh chives,
    snipped

Mayonnaise
1 cup (250 g/8 oz) whole-egg
    mayonnaise

1 tablespoon Dijon mustard
juice of 1 lemon
2 tablespoons sour cream

1 Heat 2 tablespoons of oil in a large heavy-based frying pan, add the onion and cook over medium-low heat for 40 minutes, or until soft and caramelised.
2 Cut the potatoes into large chunks (if they are small leave them whole). Cook in boiling water for 10 minutes, or until just tender, then drain and cool slightly. (Do not overcook the potatoes or they will fall apart.)
3 Grill the bacon until crisp, drain on paper towels and cool slightly before coarsely chopping.
4 Put the potato, onion and chives in a large bowl, reserving a few chives for a garnish, and mix well.
5 To make the mayonnaise, put the whole-egg mayonnaise, mustard, lemon juice and sour cream in a bowl and whisk to combine. Pour over the salad and toss to coat. Sprinkle with the bacon and garnish with the reserved chives.

NUTRITION PER SERVE
Protein 9 g; Fat 13 g; Carbohydrate 35 g; Dietary Fibre 4.5 g; Cholesterol 20 mg; 1221 kJ (292 cal)

COOK'S FILE

Note: Kipfler potatoes are small and elongated. You can also use other waxy potatoes, such as Pontiac or Desirée, and cut them into pieces.

Cook the sliced onion over medium-low heat until soft and caramelised.

Wash the potatoes and cut them into large chunks.

Whisk together the whole-egg mayonnaise, mustard, lemon juice and sour cream.

Marinated Olives

Marinated olives are delicious on their own or as part of an antipasto platter, and will generally keep refrigerated for up to 6 months. To successfully store the olives, it is important to sterilise the storage jar first by rinsing with boiling water and placing the jar in a warm oven until it is completely dry.

CITRUS HERBED OLIVES

Combine the julienned zest and juice of 1 orange and 1 lemon in a wide-necked, 750 ml (24 fl oz) sterilised jar. Add 1 tablespoon fresh thyme leaves, 2 tablespoons fresh oregano leaves, 1 crushed clove garlic and 1 tablespoon extra virgin olive oil. Seal and shake. Add 2 cups (370 g/ 12 oz) rinsed Kalamata olives and turn the jar to coat the olives, then add more oil to fully cover the olives. Marinate for 1–2 weeks in the refrigerator. Store in the refrigerator. Serve at room temperature.

LEMON AND CHILLI GREEN OLIVES

Place 2 teaspoons chopped red chilli, the julienned zest and juice of 1 lemon, 2 teaspoons sugar, 1 crushed clove garlic and 2 tablespoons extra virgin olive oil in a wide-necked, 750 ml (24 fl oz) sterilised jar. Seal and shake well to combine the ingredients. Add 2 cups (450 g/14 oz) rinsed large green olives and turn the jar to coat the olives, adding more oil to fully cover. Seal and marinate in the refrigerator for 1–2 weeks. Store in the refrigerator. Should be served at room temperature.

DILL AND LEMON OLIVES

Finely slice half a lemon and cut the slices into wedges. Rinse and drain 500 g (1 lb) Riviera or Ligurian olives. Layer the olives in a wide-necked, 750 ml (24 fl oz) sterilised jar with 3–4 sprigs fresh dill, 1 teaspoon fennel seeds, 3 finely sliced cloves garlic and the lemon wedges. Pour in the juice of half a lemon and 1^3/$_4$ cups (440 ml/14 fl oz) oil, or enough to cover the olives. Seal and marinate in the refrigerator for 1–2 weeks before using. Store in the refrigerator. Return to room temperature before serving.

SUN-DRIED TOMATO OLIVES

Rinse and drain 500 g (1 lb) black olives. Cut two slits into each olive. Layer in a wide-necked, 750 ml (24 fl oz) sterilised jar with 100 g (3½ oz) drained and chopped sun-dried tomatoes in oil (reserve the oil), 2 crushed cloves garlic, 2 bay leaves and 3 teaspoons fresh thyme leaves. Add 1 tablespoon red wine vinegar and 1 cup (250 ml/8 fl oz) oil (use the reserved sun-dried tomato oil) or enough to cover the olives. Shake well, seal and leave to marinate in the refrigerator for 1–2 weeks. Store in the refrigerator and return to room temperature before serving.

OLIVES WITH HERBS DE PROVENCE

Rinse and drain 500 g (1 lb) Niçoise or Ligurian olives. Put 1 crushed clove garlic, 2 teaspoons chopped fresh basil, 1 teaspoon each chopped fresh thyme, rosemary, marjoram, oregano

From left to right: Citrus herbed olives; Lemon and chilli green olives; Sun-dried tomato olives; Dill and lemon olives; Olives with herbs de Provence; Honey citrus olives; Lemon olives with vermouth.

and mint, 1 teaspoon fennel seeds, 2 tablespoons lemon juice and ½ cup (125 ml/4 fl oz) olive oil in a bowl and mix together. Put the olives and marinade in a wide-necked, 750 ml (24 fl oz) sterilised jar, adding extra olive oil to cover the olives. Seal and shake. Marinate in the refrigerator for 1–2 weeks. Store in the refrigerator. Serve at room temperature.

HONEY CITRUS OLIVES

Mix together the zest of 1 lemon, lime and orange, 2 tablespoons lime juice, 4 tablespoons lemon juice, 1 tablespoon orange juice, 1 tablespoon honey, 2 teaspoons wholegrain mustard, ½ cup (125 ml/4 fl oz) extra virgin olive oil, 2 thinly sliced cloves garlic, ¼ teaspoon dried oregano or 1 tablespoon chopped fresh oregano leaves and 6 thin slices of lemon and lime. Add 1½ cups (265 g/8½ oz)

drained unpitted black olives, 1½ cups (265 g/8½ oz) drained unpitted green olives, 2 tablespoons chopped fresh parsley, salt and pepper. Place in a wide-necked, 750 ml (24 fl oz) sterilised jar and seal. Shake, then marinate in the refrigerator for 1–2 weeks. Store in the refrigerator. Serve at room temperature.

LEMON OLIVES WITH VERMOUTH

Rinse and drain 340 g (11 oz) whole green or stuffed olives. Layer in a wide-necked, 750 ml (24 fl oz) sterilised jar with ½ cup (125 ml/4 fl oz) dry vermouth, 2 tablespoons lemon juice, 1 tablespoon shredded lemon rind and ⅓ cup (80 ml/2¾ fl oz) extra virgin olive oil. Shake well, seal and marinate in the refrigerator overnight. Store in the refrigerator. Return to room temperature before serving.

15

DOLMADES

Preparation time: 1 hour +
   1 hour soaking
Total cooking time: 1 hour
Makes 42

275 g (9 oz) vine leaves in brine
3/4 cup (185 ml/6 fl oz) olive oil
2 onions, finely chopped
3/4 cup (165 g/5 1/2 oz)
   short-grain rice
6 spring onions, finely chopped
1/3 cup (20 g/3/4 oz) chopped
   fresh dill
1 tablespoon chopped
   fresh mint
1 tablespoon lemon juice

1 Rinse the vine leaves in cold water, soak in warm water for 1 hour and then drain.
2 Heat 1/2 cup (125 ml/4 fl oz) of the oil in a heavy-based pan. Add the onion and cook over low heat for 5 minutes. Remove from the heat, cover and leave for 5 minutes. Add the rice, spring onion, herbs and lemon juice. Mix well and season.
3 Lay out a vine leaf, vein-side-up, on a plate. Place 3 teaspoons of filling onto the centre. Fold the sides over the mixture, then roll up towards the tip of the leaf. Repeat until you have made 42 dolmades.
4 Use five or six vine leaves to line the base of a large heavy-based pan. Pack the dolmades in the lined pan

in two layers and drizzle with the remaining oil. Put a plate on top of the dolmades, to keep them in place, and cover with 1 1/2 cups (375 ml/12 fl oz) water. Bring to the boil, reduce the heat and simmer, covered, for 45 minutes. Remove the plate, lift out the dolmades with a slotted spoon and drizzle with lemon juice. Serve either warm or cold.

NUTRITION PER DOLMADE
Protein 2 g; Fat 4.5 g; Carbohydrate 3 g; Dietary Fibre 0 g; Cholesterol 0 mg; 220 kJ (50 cal)

COOK'S FILE

Note: Fresh vine leaves can be used, if available. Use small leaves, blanched briefly in boiling water.

Put the vine leaves in a colander and rinse thoroughly under cold water.

Fold the sides of the vine leaf over the filling and roll up towards the tip of the leaf.

Cover the dolmades with a plate to keep them in place, then pour in the water.

LABNEH (YOGHURT CHEESE)

Preparation time: 20 minutes +
    4 days refrigeration
Total cooking time: Nil
Makes 24

1 kg (2 lb) thick Greek-style
    yoghurt
1½ cups (375 ml/12 fl oz)
    extra virgin olive oil
2 cloves garlic, chopped
2 tablespoons fresh rosemary
    leaves
6–8 sprigs fresh thyme

1 Put the yoghurt in a bowl and season with 2 teaspoons salt and 1 teaspoon ground pepper. Line a bowl with a piece of muslin folded in half to a 45 cm (18 inch) square. Spoon the yoghurt mixture into the centre. Bring the corners together and, using a long piece of kitchen string, tie as closely as possible to the yoghurt, leaving a loop at the end.
2 Thread the loop through the handle of a wooden spoon and hang the yoghurt over a bowl or a large jug to drain. Refrigerate for 3 days.
3 Mix the oil, garlic, rosemary and thyme sprigs together in a bowl. Untie the muslin and roll level

tablespoons of the drained yoghurt into balls (they will not be perfectly smooth). Make sure your hands are cool, and wash them after rolling a few balls. Rinse a large wide-necked jar with boiling water and dry in a warm oven. Put the labneh in the jar and cover with the herbed olive oil. Cover and refrigerate for 24 hours. Return to room temperature before serving with bread or crackers as part of an antipasto or meze platter. Store in the refrigerator for up to 1 week.

NUTRITION PER PIECE
Protein 2 g; Fat 6.5 g; Carbohydrate 2 g; Dietary Fibre 0 g; Cholesterol 6.5 mg; 312 kJ (75 cal)

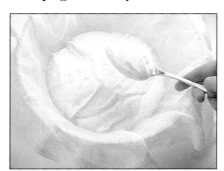

Spoon the seasoned yoghurt into the centre of the muslin square.

Thread the loop through the handle of a wooden spoon to hang the yoghurt.

With cool hands roll the drained yoghurt into balls.

CAESAR SALAD

Preparation time: 25 minutes
Total cooking time: 20 minutes
Serves 6

1 small French stick (baguette)
2 tablespoons olive oil
2 cloves garlic, halved
4 rashers bacon
2 cos lettuces
10 anchovy fillets, halved
    lengthways
1 cup (100 g/3½ oz) freshly
    shaved Parmesan
Parmesan shavings, to serve

Dressing
2 egg yolks
4 cloves garlic, crushed
1 tablespoon Dijon mustard
4 anchovy fillets
⅓ cup (80 ml/2¾ fl oz) white
    wine vinegar
2 tablespoons Worcestershire
    sauce
1¾ cups (440 ml/14 fl oz) olive oil

1 Preheat the oven to moderate 180°C (350°F/Gas 4). Cut the bread into 15 thin slices and brush both sides with oil. Bake on a baking tray for 10–15 minutes, or until golden. Cool slightly and rub each side with the cut edge of a garlic clove. Break the bread into pieces to make croûtons.
2 Trim the rind and fat from the bacon. Cook under a hot grill until crisp. Drain on paper towels until cooled, then break into chunky pieces.
3 Tear the lettuce into pieces and put in a large serving bowl with the bacon, anchovies, croûtons and Parmesan.
4 Place the egg yolks, garlic, mustard, anchovies, vinegar and Worcestershire sauce in a food processor or blender. Season and process for 20 seconds, or until smooth. With the motor running, add the oil in a thin stream until the dressing is thick and creamy. This makes enough dressing for two salads. Refrigerate the rest for up to 5 days.
5 Drizzle half the dressing over the salad and toss to combine. Sprinkle on the Parmesan shavings.

NUTRITION PER SERVE
Protein 18 g; Fat 50 g; Carbohydrate 20 g; Dietary Fibre 2 g; Cholesterol 55 mg; 2437 kJ (582 cal)

With a sharp knife, cut the anchovy fillets in half lengthways.

Rub both sides of the bread with the cut edge of the garlic clove.

Process the egg, garlic, mustard, anchovies, vinegar and Worcestershire sauce.

Add the olive oil in a thin stream until the dressing is thick and creamy.

ROASTED BALSAMIC ONIONS

Preparation time: 15 minutes +
 overnight refrigeration
Total cooking time: 1 hour 30 minutes
Serves 8 (as part of an antipasto platter)

**1 kg (2 lb) pickling onions,
 unpeeled (see Note)**
**3/4 cup (185 ml/6 fl oz) balsamic
 vinegar**
2 tablespoons soft brown sugar
3/4 cup (185 ml/6 fl oz) olive oil

1 Preheat the oven to warm 160°C
(315°F/Gas 2–3). Place the unpeeled
onions in a baking dish and roast for
1½ hours. Leave until cool enough to
handle. Trim the stems from the
onions and peel away the skin (the
outer part of the root should come
away but the onions will remain
intact). Rinse a 1-litre wide-necked
jar with boiling water and dry in a
warm oven (do not dry with a tea
towel). Add the onions to the jar.
2 Combine the vinegar and sugar in
a small screw-top jar and stir to
dissolve the sugar. Add the oil, seal
the jar and shake vigorously until
combined—the mixture will be paler
and may separate on standing.
3 Pour the vinegar mixture over the
onions, seal, and turn upside down
to coat. Marinate overnight in the
refrigerator, turning occasionally.
Return to room temperature and shake
to combine the dressing before serving.

NUTRITION PER SERVE
Protein 0.5 g; Fat 7.5 g; Carbohydrate 20 g;
Dietary Fibre 2 g; Cholesterol 0 mg;
677 kJ (162 cal)

COOK'S FILE

Note: Pickling onions are very small,
usually packed in 1 kg (2 lb) bags. The
ideal size is around 35 g (1¼ oz) each.
The sizes in the bag will probably
range from 20 g (¾ oz) up to 40 g
(1¼ oz). The cooking time given is
suitable for this range and there is no
need to cook the larger ones for any
longer. The marinating time given is a
minimum time and the onions may be
marinated for up to 3 days in the
refrigerator. The marinade may
separate after a few hours, which is
fine —simply stir occasionally.

*When cool, trim the stems from the onions
and peel away the skin.*

*Add the oil to the vinegar and sugar and
shake vigorously to combine.*

*Pour the vinegar mixture over the onions,
turning the jar to coat thoroughly.*

FRITTATA

Preparation time: 30 minutes
Total cooking time: 40 minutes
Serves 4

1½ tablespoons plain flour
4 eggs, lightly beaten
½ cup (125 ml/4 fl oz) milk
½ cup (125 ml/4 fl oz) cream
¾ cup (125 g/4 oz) cooked
    chopped silverbeet
½ cup (50 g/1¾ oz) grated
    Parmesan
2 tablespoons chopped fresh
    chives
2 tablespoons olive oil

3 Roma tomatoes
2 tablespoons shredded fresh
    basil
4 thin slices prosciutto, chopped
12 pitted black olives, sliced

1 Preheat the oven to moderately hot 200°C (400°F/Gas 6). Invert the base of a 20 cm (8 inch) springform tin so the frittata can be easily removed. Grease and line the base of the tin with baking paper. Sift the flour into a large bowl and gradually whisk in the eggs to make a smooth mixture. Add the milk, cream, silverbeet, Parmesan, chives and oil and mix until well combined. Season to taste with salt and cracked pepper.

2 Pour the mixture into the prepared tin. Halve the tomatoes lengthways, remove the seeds with a teaspoon and slice the flesh. Arrange the tomato on top of the mixture with the basil, prosciutto and olives.
3 Put the tin on a baking tray as the frittata may leak slightly, and bake for 30–40 minutes, or until puffed and golden. Loosen the frittata and leave in the tin for 10 minutes before carefully transferring to a plate. Serve warm or at room temperature as part of an antipasto platter or with salad.

NUTRITION PER SERVE
Protein 20 g; Fat 35 g; Carbohydrate 8 g; Dietary Fibre 2 g; Cholesterol 250 mg; 1712 kJ (410 cal)

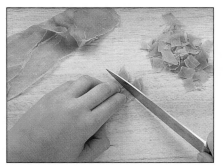

Chop the thin slices of prosciutto into small pieces.

Whisk together the eggs and the flour until smooth.

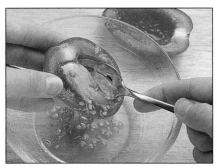

Cut the tomatoes in half lengthways and remove the seeds with a teaspoon.

LEMON PRAWN PATE

Preparation time: 30 minutes +
    1 hour refrigeration
Total cooking time: 5 minutes
Serves 6

100 g (3½ oz) unsalted butter
3 cloves garlic, crushed
750 g (1½ lb) raw prawns,
    peeled and deveined

1 teaspoon grated lemon rind
3 tablespoons lemon juice
¼ teaspoon grated nutmeg
2 tablespoons mayonnaise
2 tablespoons finely chopped
    fresh chives

1 Melt the butter in a frying pan. When it sizzles, add the garlic and prawns and cook, stirring, for 3–4 minutes, or until the prawns are opaque and cooked through. Cool.

2 Put the garlic and prawns in a food processor, add the lemon rind, juice and nutmeg. Process for 20 seconds, or until roughly puréed. Season and add the mayonnaise and chives, and process for 20 seconds, or until combined.
3 Spoon into a dish and chill for at least 1 hour, or until firm.

NUTRITION PER SERVE
Protein 25 g; Fat 17 g; Carbohydrate 2 g; Dietary Fibre 0.5 g; Cholesterol 230 mg; 1105 kJ (265 cal)

Grate the nutmeg using the fine side of a metal grater.

Cook the garlic and prawns in butter until the prawns are opaque and cook through.

Add the mayonnaise and chives, then process until well combined.

Frittata (top)
with Lemon prawn pâté

SALAMI PASTA SALAD

Preparation time: 20 minutes
Total cooking time: 10 minutes
Serves 8

1 red capsicum
1 green capsicum
4 celery sticks
1 fennel bulb, trimmed
1 red onion
200 g (6½ oz) thickly sliced
    pepper-coated salami
½ cup (15 g/½ oz) chopped
    fresh flat-leaf parsley
300 g (10 oz) mixed coloured
    fettucine, broken into shorter
    pieces

Dressing
½ cup (125 ml/4 fl oz) olive oil
3 tablespoons lemon juice
2½ tablespoons Dijon mustard
1 teaspoon sugar
1 clove garlic, crushed

1 Slice the red and green capsicums into strips and place them in a large bowl. Slice the celery and add to the bowl. Cut the fennel and onion in half, then slice and add to the bowl. Cut the salami into strips and add to the bowl along with the parsley.
2 Cook the fettucine in a large pan of rapidly boiling salted water until just tender. Drain and rinse in cold water. Transfer the cooked pasta to the bowl and mix thoroughly with the capsicum,
celery, fennel, onion, parsley and salami.
3 To make the dressing, combine the olive oil, lemon juice, mustard, sugar and crushed garlic, and season to taste with salt and plenty of cracked pepper. Pour over the salad and toss well to coat.

NUTRITION PER SERVE
Protein 10 g; Fat 25 g; Carbohydrate 30 g; Dietary Fibre 2.5 g; Cholesterol 26 mg; 1599 kJ (380 cal)

COOK'S FILE

Storage time: This salad will keep for 1–2 days in an airtight container in the refrigerator.
Variation: Other types of salami may be used if you prefer, such as those flavoured with chilli or garlic.

Use a sharp knife to halve the fennel and then cut into slices.

Cut the salami into strips and add to the bowl along with the chopped parsley.

To make the dressing, put the ingredients in a bowl and mix together with a fork.

SMOKY TOMATO SAUCE

Preparation time: 15 minutes
Total cooking time: 35–45 minutes
Makes about 1 litre

Smoking Mix
2 tablespoons Chinese or
    Ceylon tea leaves
2 star anise, crushed
1 strip orange rind
1/2 teaspoon five-spice powder
6 juniper berries, crushed

2 onions, quartered
2 red capsicums, cut into
    large pieces
2 red chillies, cut in half
3 tablespoons oil
3 cloves garlic, chopped
500 g (1 lb) tomatoes, chopped
2 tablespoons Worcestershire
    sauce
1/2 cup (125 ml/4 fl oz) barbecue
    sauce
2 tablespoons tamarind
    concentrate
1 tablespoon white vinegar
1 tablespoon soft brown sugar

1 Combine all the ingredients for the smoking mix in a small bowl. Pour the mix into the centre of a sheet of foil and fold the edges to prevent the mix from spreading. (This will form an open container to allow the mix to smoke.) Place the foil container on the bottom of a dry wok or wide frying pan. Place an open rack or steamer in the wok or frying pan, making sure it is elevated over the mix.
2 Place the onion, capsicum and chilli onto the rack and cover with a lid, or alternatively cover the entire wok or frying pan tightly with foil to prevent the smoke from escaping.
3 Smoke over medium heat for 10–15 minutes, or until the vegetables are tender. If you prefer a very smoky sauce cook the vegetables for longer, if you prefer it less so, reduce the time. Remove the container with the smoking mix.
4 Dice the onion, capsicum and chilli quite finely. Heat the oil in the wok and add the garlic and cooked vegetables. Fry over medium heat for 3 minutes, then add the tomato and cook until pulpy. Add the sauces, tamarind, vinegar and sugar. Simmer, stirring occasionally, for 20–25 minutes, or until the sauce is quite thick. Serve with meat, fish or as a pasta sauce. Store in the refrigerator.

NUTRITION PER TABLESPOON
Protein 0.5 g; Fat 1.5 g; Carbohydrate 2.5 g; Dietary Fibre 0.5 g; Cholesterol 0 mg; 90 kJ (20 cal)

COOK'S FILE

Note: For a smoother sauce, process in a food processor for about 30 seconds.

Fold the edges of the foil to form an open container that allows the mix to smoke.

Place the open rack in the wok or frying pan then put on the onion, capsicum and chilli.

Add the tamarind concentrate to the sauce and simmer.

CHARGRILLED VEGETABLE TERRINE

Preparation time: 30 minutes +
overnight refrigeration
Total cooking time: Nil
Serves 8

350 g (11 oz) ricotta
2 cloves garlic, crushed
8 large slices chargrilled
eggplant, drained
10 slices chargrilled red
capsicum, drained
8 slices chargrilled zucchini,
drained
45 g (1 1/2 oz) rocket leaves
3 marinated artichokes,
drained and sliced
85 g (3 oz) semi-dried tomatoes,
drained and chopped
100 g (3 1/2 oz) marinated
mushrooms, drained and
halved

1 Line a 23 1/2 x 13 x 6 1/2 cm (9 x 5 x 2 1/2 inch) loaf tin with plastic wrap, leaving a generous amount hanging over the sides. Place the ricotta and garlic in a bowl and beat until smooth. Season well and set aside.
2 Line the base of the tin with half the eggplant, cutting and fitting to cover the base. Top with a layer of half the capsicum, then all the zucchini slices. Spread evenly with the ricotta mixture and press down firmly. Place the rocket leaves on top of the ricotta. Arrange the artichoke, tomato and mushrooms in three rows lengthways on top of the ricotta.
3 Top with another layer of capsicum and finish with the eggplant. Cover securely with the overlapping plastic wrap. Put a piece of cardboard on top

and weigh it down with weights or small food cans. Refrigerate overnight.
4 To serve, peel back the plastic wrap and turn the terrine out onto a plate. Remove the plastic wrap and cut into thick slices.

NUTRITION PER SERVE
Protein 6 g; Fat 5 g; Carbohydrate 3 g; Dietary Fibre 2 g; Cholesterol 20 mg; 350 kJ (85 cal)

COOK'S FILE

Note: You can buy chargrilled vegetables and marinated mushrooms and artichokes at your local deli. Or make your own by following the recipes on pages 9, 42 and 65.
Storage time: Cover any leftovers with plastic wrap and store in the refrigerator for up to 2 days.

Put the ricotta and crushed garlic in a bowl and beat until smooth.

Arrange the mushrooms, tomato and artichoke in three rows over the rocket.

Cover the terrine with cardboard and weigh down with small food cans.

Use a sharp knife to cut the smoked salmon into thin strips.

Put the cream cheese, mustards, lemon juice and dill in a bowl and mix well.

Using a spoon, flatten the centre of each pastry before returning to the oven.

Spread the cream cheese mixture onto the cooled pastries.

SMOKED SALMON TARTLETS

Preparation time: 30 minutes +
  10 minutes refrigeration
Total cooking time: 30 minutes
Makes 24

250 g (8 oz) cream cheese,
  at room temperature
1½ tablespoons wholegrain
  mustard
2 teaspoons Dijon mustard
2 tablespoons lemon juice
2 tablespoons chopped
  fresh dill
6 sheets ready-rolled puff
  pastry
300 g (10 oz) smoked salmon,
  cut into thin strips
65 g (2¼ oz) jar baby capers
fresh dill sprigs, to decorate

1 Preheat the oven to hot 210°C (415°F/Gas 6–7). Line a large baking tray with baking paper. Mix together the cream cheese, mustards, lemon juice and dill. Cover and refrigerate.
2 Cut four 9.5 cm (3¾ inch) rounds from each sheet of pastry with a fluted cutter and place on the prepared baking tray. Prick the pastries all over. Cover and refrigerate for 10 minutes.
3 Bake in batches for 7 minutes, remove from the oven and use a spoon to flatten the centre of each pastry. Return to the oven and bake for a further 5 minutes, or until the pastry is golden. Allow to cool, then spread a rounded teaspoon of the cream cheese mixture over each pastry, leaving a 1 cm (½ inch) border. Arrange the salmon over the top. Decorate with a few capers and a sprig of dill.

NUTRITION PER SERVE
Protein 6 g; Fat 15 g; Carbohydrate 15 g;
Dietary Fibre 0.5 g; Cholesterol 25 mg;
869 kJ (210 cal)

Dips

These exotic dips are full of flavour and quick and easy to make. They are always popular at parties served with raw vegetables and crackers, and are a delicious accompaniment to breads and cold meats at a lazy Sunday picnic.

TARAMASALATA

Remove the crusts from 4 slices of white bread. Soak in 1/4 cup (60 ml/ 2 fl oz) milk for 5 minutes, then remove, squeezing out the excess liquid. Process 100 g (31/2 oz) smoked cod's roe (tarama) and 1 egg yolk in a food processor for 10 seconds. Add the bread, 1 crushed clove garlic and 1 tablespoon grated onion. Process for 20 seconds, or until the mixture is well combined and smooth. With the motor running, gradually add 1/4 cup (60 ml/ 2 fl oz) olive oil in a thin stream.

Process until all the oil is absorbed. Add 1/3 cup (80 ml/23/4 fl oz) lemon juice in small amounts, to taste. Serve with bread and black olives. Makes 1 cup (220 g/7 oz). Keep in an airtight container in the refrigerator for 2–3 days. Return to room temperature before serving.

SKORDALIA

Place 1 cup (250 g/8 oz) mayonnaise and 1 cup (250 g/ 8 oz) Greek-style yoghurt in a bowl and beat with a wooden spoon. Add 100 g (31/2 oz)

ground almonds, 2 crushed cloves garlic and 1/2 cup (40 g/11/4 oz) fresh breadcrumbs and stir until well combined. Fold through 3 finely sliced spring onions, 2 tablespoons each finely chopped fresh parsley and finely chopped fresh chives, 1 teaspoon finely grated lemon rind and 1 tablespoon lemon juice. Season. Spoon into a serving dish, cover and refrigerate until serving. Serve with raw vegetables and grilled Turkish bread. Makes about 2 cups (500 g/ 16 oz). Keep in an airtight container in the refrigerator for 2–3 days.

BABA GANOUJ (eggplant dip)

Preheat the oven to moderate 180°C (350°F/Gas 4). Cut 2 eggplants in half lengthways, sprinkle with salt and leave for 20 minutes. Rinse and pat dry with a paper towel. Bake the eggplants for 35 minutes, or until soft. Remove the skin. Place the flesh in a food processor with 3–4 crushed cloves garlic, 2 tablespoons lemon juice, 2 tablespoons tahini and 1 tablespoon olive oil. Season to taste. Process for 20–30 seconds, then sprinkle with paprika and serve with Lebanese bread. Makes 2 cups (500 g/ 16 oz). Keep in an airtight container in the refrigerator for 2–3 days.

AIOLI

Put 2 egg yolks in a food processor with 2 teaspoons lemon juice, 3 chopped cloves garlic, 1/4 teaspoon salt and a little cracked black pepper.

From left to right: Taramasalata; Skordalia; Baba ganouj; Smoked trout dip; Hummus; Aioli.

Process for about 10 seconds, or until blended. While the motor is still running, slowly add 1 cup (250 ml/ 8 fl oz) olive oil in a slow stream until the mixture is thick and creamy. Add another 3 teaspoons lemon juice and season to taste. Pour into a serving bowl and scatter with 2 teaspoons fresh chopped parsley. Serve with boiled vegetables, cold cooked chicken and fish. Makes 1 1/2 cups (375 g/ 12 oz). Keep for up to 3 days in an airtight container in the refrigerator.

SMOKED TROUT DIP

Remove the skin and bones from 250 g (8 oz) smoked trout and flake the flesh. Put the flesh in a blender or food processor and add 1 1/2 teaspoons olive oil, 2 teaspoons cream and 1 tablespoon lemon juice. Blend until a thick paste forms. Add 1/3 cup (80 ml/2 3/4 fl oz)

cream, a little at a time, and process (don't curdle the cream). Season. Place in a bowl. Combine 1 tablespoon each chopped pistachios and chopped fresh parsley. Sprinkle over the dip and serve with witlof leaves or cucumber sticks. Makes about 1 cup (250 g/8 oz). Keep in an airtight container in the refrigerator for 2–3 days.

HUMMUS

Drain a 425 g (14 oz) can chickpeas and place in a food processor with 2 tablespoons olive oil, 2 crushed cloves garlic and 2–3 tablespoons lemon juice. Season. Process for 20–30 seconds, or until smooth. Add 1/4 cup (65 g/2 1/4 oz) tahini and process for 10 seconds. Serve with Lebanese bread. Makes 1 cup (250 g/ 8 oz). Will keep for up to 3 days in an airtight container in the refrigerator.

CHICKEN LIVER PATE WITH PISTACHIO NUTS AND PROSCIUTTO

Preparation time: 20 minutes +
3 hours refrigeration
Total cooking time: 15 minutes
Serves 10

6 very thin slices prosciutto
2 tablespoons butter
3 tablespoons olive oil
80 g (2¾ oz) finely diced bacon
1 onion, finely chopped
2 cloves garlic, crushed
500 g (1 lb) chicken livers
3 bay leaves
⅓ cup (80 ml/2¾ fl oz) sherry
or brandy
125 g (4 oz) butter, softened
⅓ cup (50 g/1¾ oz) pistachio
nuts, toasted

1 Line a 1.5 litre loaf tin with foil. Then line with the prosciutto so that it hangs over the sides, making sure each slice overlaps. Heat the butter and oil and cook the bacon, onion and garlic for 5–6 minutes, or until the onion is softened but not browned.

2 Trim the chicken livers of any fat and veins. Add them to the pan with the bay leaves. Increase the heat to hot and cook for 3–4 minutes, or until the livers are brown on the outside, but still pink on the inside.

3 Add the sherry and simmer, stirring continuously, for 3 minutes, or until the liquid has almost disappeared. Remove the bay leaves. Put the mixture in a food processor and blend to a very fine texture. Gradually add the butter and blend until smooth. Season, then stir in the pistachios.

4 Spoon the pâté mixture into the tin and fold the prosciutto over the top to enclose it. Refrigerate for at least 3 hours before serving. Cut into slices to serve.

NUTRITION PER SERVE
Protein 4 g; Fat 20 g; Carbohydrate 2 g;
Dietary Fibre 0.5 g; Cholesterol 48 mg;
938 kJ (224 cal)

COOK'S FILE

Note: The flavour, colour and texture of the pâté will improve after 2 days, and it will also become easier to slice. Keep refrigerated for 3–4 days.

Line the tin with the prosciutto with each slice overlapping.

Remove the fat and veins from the chicken livers before cooking.

Add the sherry and simmer until most of the liquid has disappeared.

Stir the toasted pistachio nuts through the liver mixture.

ARANCINI (RICE CROQUETTES)

Preparation time: 45 minutes +
  10 minutes soaking + 1 hour
  refrigeration
Total cooking time: 1 hour
Makes 10

2 cups (440 g/14 oz) short-grain
   rice
1 egg, lightly beaten
1 egg yolk
1/2 cup (50 g/13/4 oz) grated
   Parmesan

Meat Sauce
1 dried porcini mushroom
1 tablespoon olive oil
1 onion, chopped
125 g (4 oz) minced beef or veal
2 slices prosciutto, finely
   chopped
2 tablespoons tomato paste
1/3 cup (80 ml/23/4 fl oz) white
   wine
1/2 teaspoon dried thyme leaves
3 tablespoons finely chopped
   fresh parsley

plain flour
2 eggs, lightly beaten
dry breadcrumbs, for coating
oil, for deep-frying

1 Cook the rice in boiling water for 20 minutes, or until just soft. Drain, without rinsing, and cool. Put in a large bowl and add the egg, egg yolk and Parmesan. Stir until the rice sticks together. Cover and set aside.
2 To make the meat sauce, soak the mushroom in hot water for 10 minutes to soften, then squeeze dry and chop finely. Heat the oil in a frying pan.

Add the mushroom and onion and cook for 3 minutes, or until soft. Add the mince and cook, stirring, until browned. Add the prosciutto, tomato paste, wine, thyme and pepper to taste. Cook, stirring, for 5 minutes, or until all the liquid is absorbed. Stir in the parsley and set aside to cool.
3 With wet hands, form the rice mixture into 10 balls. Wet your hands again and gently pull the balls apart. Place 3 teaspoons of the meat sauce in the centre of each. Reshape to enclose

the filling. Roll in the flour, beaten egg and breadcrumbs and chill for 1 hour.
4 Fill a deep heavy-based pan one third full of oil and heat until a cube of bread browns in 15 seconds. Deep-fry the croquettes in oil, two at a time, for 3–4 minutes, or until golden brown. Drain on paper towels and keep warm while cooking the rest.

NUTRITION PER ARANCINI
Protein 9 g; Fat 8.5 g; Carbohydrate 37 g;
Dietary Fibre 2.5 g; Cholesterol 80 mg;
1135 kJ (270 cal)

Soak the dried mushroom in hot water, then squeeze dry and chop finely.

Gently pull the balls of rice apart and fill with 3 teaspoons of meat sauce.

Reshape the balls and roll them in the flour, egg and breadcrumbs.

PISSALADIERE

Preparation time: 50 minutes +
   40 minutes standing
Total cooking time: 2 hours
Serves 8

7 g (¼ oz) dried yeast
1 teaspoon caster sugar
2½ cups (310 g/10 oz) plain
   flour
2 tablespoons powdered milk
1 tablespoon oil

Tomato and Onion Topping
⅓ cup (80 ml/2¾ fl oz) olive oil
3–4 cloves garlic, finely chopped
6 onions, cut into thin rings
425 g (14 oz) can chopped
   tomatoes
1 tablespoon tomato paste
¼ cup (15 g/½ oz) chopped
   fresh parsley
1 tablespoon chopped fresh
   thyme
olive oil, for brushing
3 x 45 g (1½ oz) cans anchovy
   fillets, drained and halved
   lengthways
36 small black olives

1 Lightly grease two 30 cm (12 inch) pizza trays. Place the yeast, sugar and 1 cup (250 ml/8 fl oz) of warm water in a small bowl. Set aside in a warm place for 5–10 minutes, or until frothy. Sift 2 cups (250 g/8 oz) of the plain flour, ½ teaspoon salt and the milk powder into a large bowl and make a well in the centre. Add the oil and frothy yeast and mix together thoroughly.
2 Turn out onto a lightly floured surface and knead for 10 minutes, gradually adding small amounts of the remaining flour, until the dough is smooth and elastic. Place in an oiled bowl and brush the surface with a little oil, cover with plastic wrap and set aside in a warm place for 30 minutes, or until doubled in size.

3 To make the topping, heat the oil in a heavy-based pan. Add the garlic and onion and cook, covered, over low heat for about 40 minutes, stirring frequently. The onion should be softened but not browned. Remove the lid and cook, stirring frequently, for a further 30 minutes, or until lightly golden. Take care not to burn. Set aside to cool.

4 Cook the chopped tomato in a pan, stirring frequently, for 20 minutes, or until thick and reduced to about 1 cup (250 ml/8 fl oz). Remove from the heat and stir in the tomato paste and herbs. Add some cracked black pepper. Cool, then stir into the cooled onion mixture.

5 Preheat the oven to hot 220°C (425°F/Gas 7). Punch down the dough, then turn out onto a lightly floured surface and knead for 2 minutes. Divide the dough in half. Return one portion to the bowl and cover. Roll the other portion out to a 30 cm (12 inch) circle and press evenly into the prepared tin. Brush with some olive oil. Spread half the onion and tomato mixture evenly onto the dough, leaving a small border. Arrange half the anchovy fillets over the top in a lattice pattern and place an olive in each square. Repeat with the rest of the dough and topping. Bake for 15–20 minutes, or until the dough is cooked through and lightly browned.

NUTRITION PER SERVE
Protein 9 g; Fat 17 g; Carbohydrate 35 g; Dietary Fibre 4.75 g; Cholesterol 7.5 mg; 1390 kJ (330 cal)

Pour the oil and frothy yeast into the flour mixture and mix thoroughly.

Cook the onion over low heat until it has softened but not browned.

Stir the tomato paste and herbs into the cooked tomatoes.

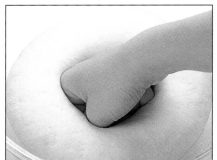

Punch down the dough to expel any excess air before kneading.

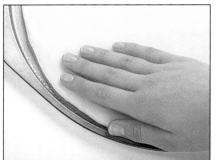

Press one portion of dough evenly into the prepared tin and brush with olive oil.

Arrange half of the anchovy fillets in a lattice pattern over the top.

ORANGE POPPY SEED ROASTED VEGETABLES

Preparation time: 20 minutes
Total cooking time: 50 minutes
Serves 6

500 g (1 lb) new potatoes, unpeeled, quartered
6 parsnips, quartered lengthways
500 g (1 lb) orange sweet potato, cut into large pieces
335 g (11 oz) baby carrots, with some of the tops left on
6 pickling onions, halved

1/3 cup (80 ml/2³/4 fl oz) oil
2 tablespoons poppy seeds
200 g (6¹/2 oz) triple cream Brie, thinly sliced

Orange Dressing
1/2 cup (125 ml/4 fl oz) orange juice
2 cloves garlic, crushed
1 tablespoon Dijon mustard
1 teaspoon white wine vinegar
1 teaspoon sesame oil

1 Preheat the oven to moderately hot 200°C (400°F/Gas 6). Put the potato, parsnip, sweet potato, carrots, pickling onions and oil in a large, deep baking dish. Toss the vegetables to coat with the oil.

2 Bake for 50 minutes, or until the vegetables are crisp and tender, tossing every 15 minutes. Sprinkle with the poppy seeds.

3 To make the orange dressing, whisk together the orange juice, garlic, mustard, vinegar and oil. Pour the dressing over the warm vegetables and toss to coat. Transfer to a serving dish, top with the Brie and serve while still warm.

NUTRITION PER SERVE
Protein 6.5 g; Fat 15 g; Carbohydrate 40 g; Dietary Fibre 8.5 g; Cholesterol 0 mg; 1325 kJ (315 cal)

Use a sharp knife to cut the Brie into thin slices.

Put the vegetables in a baking dish with the oil and toss to coat.

To make the dressing, put the ingredients in a bowl and mix together with a fork.

STUFFED CHICKEN BREASTS

Preparation time: 40 minutes
Total cooking time: 45 minutes
Serves 6

1 tablespoon olive oil
1 onion, finely chopped
2 cloves garlic, crushed
100 g (3¹/₂ oz) ham, finely
    chopped
1 green capsicum, finely
    chopped
2 tablespoons finely chopped
    pitted black olives

¹/₃ cup (35 g/1¹/₄ oz) grated
    Parmesan
6 chicken breast fillets
plain flour, to coat
2 eggs, lightly beaten
1¹/₂ cups (150 g/5 oz) dry
    breadcrumbs
¹/₄ cup (60 ml/2 fl oz) olive oil

1 Heat the oil in a pan and add the onion, garlic, ham and capsicum. Cook, stirring, over medium heat for 5 minutes, or until the onion is soft. Remove and place in a heatproof bowl.
2 Add the olives and Parmesan. Cut a deep pocket in the side of each fillet, cutting almost through to the other side.

3 Fill each fillet with the ham mixture and secure with toothpicks along the opening of the pocket. Coat each fillet with the flour, shaking off any excess. Dip into the beaten egg and then coat with the breadcrumbs. Heat the oil in a large pan and cook the fillets, in batches, over medium–high heat for 15–20 minutes, turning half way through, until golden and cooked through. To serve, remove the toothpicks, then cut diagonally into thin slices.

NUTRITION PER SERVE
Protein 35 g; Fat 20 g; Carbohydrate 20 g; Dietary Fibre 2 g; Cholesterol 115 mg; 1660 kJ (395 cal)

Cut a deep pocket in the side of each fillet, cutting almost through to the other side.

Spoon the filling into each fillet, securing the pocket openings with toothpicks.

Coat the chicken breasts in the beaten egg and breadcrumbs before cooking.

SPINACH AND FETA TRIANGLES

Preparation time: 30 minutes
Total cooking time: 40 minutes
Makes 8

1 kg (2 lb) English spinach
1/4 cup (60 ml/2 fl oz) olive oil
1 onion, chopped
10 spring onions, sliced
1/3 cup (20 g/3/4 oz) chopped
    fresh parsley
1 tablespoon chopped fresh dill
large pinch of ground nutmeg
1/3 cup (35 g/11/4 oz) freshly
    grated Parmesan
150 g (5 oz) crumbled feta
90 g (3 oz) ricotta
4 eggs, lightly beaten
40 g (11/4 oz) butter, melted
1 tablespoon olive oil, extra
12 sheets filo pastry

1 Trim any coarse stems from the spinach. Wash the leaves thoroughly, roughly chop and place in a large pan with just a little water clinging to the leaves. Cover and cook gently over low heat for 5 minutes, or until the leaves have wilted. Drain well and allow to cool slightly before squeezing tightly to remove the excess water.
2 Heat the oil in a heavy-based frying pan. Add the onion and cook over low heat for 10 minutes, or until tender and golden. Add the spring onion and cook for a further 3 minutes. Remove from the heat. Stir in the drained spinach, parsley, dill, nutmeg, Parmesan, feta, ricotta and egg. Season well.
3 Preheat the oven to moderate 180°C (350°F/Gas 4). Grease two baking trays. Combine the melted

butter with the extra oil. Work with three sheets of pastry at a time, keeping the rest covered with a damp tea towel. Brush each sheet with butter mixture and lay them on top of each other. Cut in half lengthways.
4 Place 4 tablespoons of the filling on an angle at the end of each strip. Fold the pastry over to enclose the filling and form a triangle. Continue folding the triangle over until your reach the end of the pastry. Put the triangles on the baking trays and brush with the remaining butter mixture. Bake for 20–25 minutes, or until the pastry is golden brown.

NUTRITION PER TRIANGLE
Protein 15 g; Fat 25 g; Carbohydrate 10 g; Dietary Fibre 4.5 g; Cholesterol 125 mg; 1325 kJ (315 cal)

COOK'S FILE

Note: Feta is a traditional Greek-style salty cheese that should be stored immersed in lightly salted water and kept refrigerated. Rinse and pat dry before using.
Variation: If you are unable to buy English spinach, silverbeet can be used instead. Use the same quantity and trim the coarse white stems from the leaves.

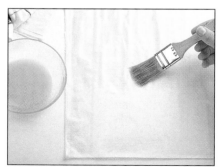

Brush each sheet of filo pastry with the butter mixture.

Fold the pastry over the spinach mixture to form a triangle.

Continue folding the triangle over until you reach the end of the pastry sheet.

CAMEMBERT AND POTATO TERRINE

Preparation time: 1 hour + overnight refrigeration
Total cooking time: 50 minutes
Serves 8

1 kg (2 lb) new potatoes, unpeeled
3 Granny Smith apples
125 g (4 oz) butter
3 tablespoons olive oil
200 g (6½ oz) Camembert, chilled and very thinly sliced
2 tablespoons chopped fresh parsley

1 Boil the potatoes in salted water for about 15 minutes, or until soft. Drain and cool, then peel and cut into slices 1 cm (½ inch) thick. Core and slice the apples into 5 mm (¼ inch) thick rounds. Heat half the butter and half the oil in a pan and cook the potato until just golden. Drain on paper towels. Heat the remaining butter and oil. Lightly fry the apple until golden. Drain on paper towels.

2 Line a 25 x 11 cm (10 x 4½ inch) terrine with baking paper. Preheat the oven to moderate 180°C (350°F/Gas 4).

3 Arrange a layer of potato in the base of the terrine. Add a layer of apple and then Camembert. Sprinkle with the parsley and season well with salt and cracked pepper. Build up the layers, finishing with potato.

4 Lightly oil a piece of foil and cover the terrine, sealing well. Put the terrine in a baking dish and half fill the dish with water. Bake for 20 minutes. Remove from the oven and cover with a piece of cardboard. Put weights or food cans on top of the cardboard to compress the terrine. Refrigerate overnight. Turn out and cut into slices to serve.

NUTRITION PER SERVE
Protein 8 g; Fat 25 g; Carbohydrate 20 g; Dietary Fibre 3 g; Cholesterol 65 mg; 1456 kJ (350 cal)

Slice the apples into thick rounds and fry in butter and oil until golden.

Put the potato, apple and Camembert into the terrine in layers.

Cover the cooked terrine with cardboard and top with evenly spaced food cans.

TOMATO, PARMESAN AND ANCHOVY TARTS

Preparation time: 10 minutes +
   30 minutes cooling
Total cooking time: 1 hour
   35 minutes
Serves 10

3 tablespoons olive oil
1 onion, finely chopped
2 x 800 g (1 lb 10 oz) cans
   tomatoes
2 tablespoons finely chopped
   fresh flat-leaf parsley
1 teaspoon dried basil
1 teaspoon sugar
2 sheets ready-rolled
   shortcrust pastry
2 teaspoons finely chopped
   anchovy fillets
2 tablespoons grated Parmesan
3 eggs, lightly beaten

1 Heat the oil in a frying pan and gently fry the onion over medium heat for 15 minutes, or until golden. Drain the tomatoes and chop into a pulp. Drain off any remaining liquid. Add the parsley, basil and sugar and cook for 20–30 seconds, stirring constantly.
2 Add the tomatoes, then reduce the heat and simmer for 30 minutes, or until darkened and quite dry. Leave to cool for 30 minutes.
3 Preheat the oven to moderate 180°C (350°F/Gas 4) and grease two 20 cm (8 inch) shallow fluted loose-based flan tins. Line each tin with a sheet of pastry and sparsely prick the bottom with a fork. Line with baking paper, fill with baking beads and bake for 10 minutes. Remove the baking paper and bead. Bake for a further 10 minutes, or until the base is dry.

4 Stir the anchovies, Parmesan and eggs through the filling, then put into the pastry cases and level the surfaces. Bake for 30 minutes, or until set.

NUTRITION PER SERVE
Protein 6 g; Fat 17 g; Carbohydrate 18 g; Dietary Fibre 2 g; Cholesterol 65 mg; 1045 kJ (250 cal)

Drain the tomatoes and roughly chop them into a pulp.

Line each tin with pastry and prick the bottom with a fork to reduce puffing.

Add the chopped anchovies, Parmesan and eggs to the filling mixture.

ASHED HERBED GOAT'S CHEESE

Preparation time: 15 minutes +
  overnight refrigeration
Total cooking time: 20 minutes
Serves 8

4 sprigs fresh sage
4 sprigs fresh rosemary
4 sprigs fresh thyme

4 sprigs fresh marjoram
4 x 100 g (3¹/2 oz) goat's cheese
  rounds or logs

1 Place the sage, rosemary, thyme and marjoram in a small pan. Cover and dry-cook over medium heat for 20 minutes without removing the lid. Remove from the heat and leave, covered, for 5 minutes. The herbs will be blackened. Transfer to a food processor and finely chop.

2 Place the goat's cheese on paper towels and pat dry. Spread the ash out on a large plate. Roll the goat's cheese in the ashed herbs to coat evenly. Cover with plastic wrap and refrigerate overnight. Serve as part of a cheese or antipasto platter, or toss through a salad.

NUTRITION PER SERVE
Protein 10 g; Fat 16 g; Carbohydrate 0 g;
Dietary Fibre 0 g; Cholesterol 50 mg;
775 kJ (185 cal)

After the herbs have been dry-cooked they will be blackened.

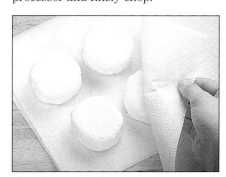

Put the goat's cheese on paper towels and pat dry.

Roll the goat's cheeses in the blackened herbs before refrigerating overnight.

CHICKPEA AND ROAST VEGETABLE SALAD

Preparation time: 25 minutes +
30 minutes standing
Total cooking time: 40 minutes
Serves 8

500 g (1 lb) butternut pumpkin,
cubed
2 red capsicums, halved
4 slender eggplants, sliced in
half lengthways
4 zucchini, sliced in half
lengthways
4 onions, quartered

olive oil, for brushing
2 x 300 g (10 oz) cans
chickpeas, rinsed and drained
2 tablespoons chopped fresh
flat-leaf parsley

Dressing
1/3 cup (80 ml/2 3/4 fl oz) olive oil
2 tablespoons lemon juice
1 clove garlic, crushed
1 tablespoon chopped fresh thyme

1 Preheat the oven to hot 220°C
(425°F/Gas 7). Brush two baking trays
with oil and lay out the vegetables in
a single layer. Brush lightly with the
olive oil.

2 Bake for 40 minutes, or until the
vegetables are tender and begin to
brown slightly on the edges. Cool.
Remove the skins from the capsicum
if you want. Chop the capsicum,
eggplant and zucchini into pieces,
then put the vegetables in a bowl with
the chickpeas and half the parsley.
3 Whisk together all the dressing
ingredients in a bowl. Season, then
toss through the vegetables. Set aside
for 30 minutes and sprinkle with the
rest of the parsley before serving.

NUTRITION PER SERVE
Protein 8.5 g; Fat 12 g; Carbohydrate 20 g;
Dietary Fibre 7.5 g; Cholesterol 0 mg;
935 kJ (225 cal)

Rinse the chickpeas under cold water then drain thoroughly.

Chop the roasted capsicum, eggplant and zucchini into small pieces.

Put the olive oil, lemon juice, garlic and thyme into a bowl and whisk to combine.

Process the flour, butter and iced water until the mixture just comes together.

Turn the pastry out onto a lightly floured surface and gather into a ball.

Line the flan tin with the pastry and trim off any excess with a sharp knife.

Once the pastry has cooled, gently spread the onion mixture over the base.

QUICHE LORRAINE

Preparation time: 45 minutes +
  30 minutes refrigeration
Total cooking time: 1 hour
Serves 6

1¹/₃ cups (165 g/5¹/₂ oz) plain
  flour
130 g (4¹/₂ oz) butter, chilled
  and chopped
1 onion, finely chopped
3 rashers bacon, rind removed,
  finely chopped
3 eggs, lightly beaten
³/₄ cup (185 ml/6 fl oz) cream
80 g (2³/₄ oz) Gruyère, grated
¹/₄ teaspoon ground nutmeg

1 Place the flour and 100 g (3¹/₂ oz) of the butter in a food processor and pulse for 15 seconds, or until crumbly. Add 2 tablespoons of iced water and process in short bursts until the mixture just comes together (add 1 more tablespoon of water if needed). Turn out onto a floured surface and gather into a ball. Cover in plastic wrap and refrigerate for 20 minutes.
2 Melt the remaining butter in a heavy-based frying pan and cook the onion and bacon over medium heat for 10 minutes, stirring occasionally.
3 Preheat the oven to moderate 180°C (350°F/Gas 4). Roll out the pastry on a lightly floured surface. Line a 23 cm (9 inch) shallow round flan tin with the pastry and trim off any excess. Refrigerate for 10 minutes. Line with crumpled baking paper and fill with baking beads or rice, then bake for 10 minutes. Remove the paper and beads and bake for 10 minutes, or until the base is dry and cooked. Cool.
4 Spread the onion mixture over the base. Whisk together the eggs, cream and half the cheese. Season. Pour into the pastry case and sprinkle on the remaining cheese and the nutmeg. Bake for 30 minutes, or until just firm.

NUTRITION PER SERVE
Protein 13 g; Fat 35 g; Carbohydrate 20 g; Dietary Fibre 1.5 g; Cholesterol 120 mg; 1940 kJ (465 cal)

RED CAPSICUM RELISH

Preparation time: 40 minutes +
a few weeks standing
Total cooking time: 1 hour 45 minutes
Fills three 250 ml (8 fl oz) jars

1 kg (2 lb) red capsicums
1 teaspoon black peppercorns
2 teaspoons black mustard
seeds
2 red onions, thinly sliced
4 cloves garlic, chopped
1½ cups (375 ml/12 fl oz) red
wine vinegar
2 apples, peeled, cored and
grated
1 teaspoon grated fresh ginger
1 cup (230 g/7½ oz) soft brown
sugar

1 Cut the capsicums into quarters, remove the seeds and membrane and thinly slice. Tie the peppercorns in a piece of muslin and secure with string. Combine the capsicum, peppercorns, mustard seeds, onion, garlic, vinegar, apple and ginger in a large pan. Simmer for 30 minutes, or until the capsicum is soft.

2 Add the sugar and stir over low heat until completely dissolved. Simmer, stirring occasionally, for 1¼ hours, or until the relish has reduced and thickened. Remove the muslin bag.

3 Rinse the jars with boiling water then dry in a warm oven. Spoon the relish into the hot jars and seal. Turn the jars upside down for 2 minutes, then turn them the other way up and leave to cool. Label and date. Allow the flavours to develop for a few weeks before using. Will keep in a cool dark place for up to 1 year. Refrigerate after opening.

NUTRITION PER TABLESPOON
Protein 0.5 g; Fat 0 g; Carbohydrate 85 g;
Dietary Fibre 0.5 g; Cholesterol 0 mg;
160 kJ (40 cal)

COOK'S FILE

Serving suggestion: Serve with a selection of meats or cheeses.

Put the peppercorns in the centre of a piece of muslin and tie with string.

Add the brown sugar to the capsicum mixture and stir over heat until dissolved.

Spoon the thickened relish into the sterilised jars and seal.

LEEK AND CAPER SALAD

Preparation time: 10 minutes +
   10 minutes cooling
Total cooking time: 20 minutes
Serves 6 as an accompaniment

5 leeks, trimmed
1/3 cup (80 ml/2³/4 fl oz) extra
   virgin olive oil
2 tablespoons sherry vinegar

2 tablespoons baby capers,
   drained and rinsed

1 Cut the leeks in half lengthways
and wash under cold running water.
Cut them into 5 cm lengths, then cut
in half again lengthways. Heat the oil
in a large heavy-based pan, add the
leeks and stir until covered with the
oil. Cover and cook over low heat for
15–20 minutes, or until the leeks
are soft and tender (but don't let them

brown or burn). Set aside to cool for
10 minutes.
2 Stir through the vinegar and season
to taste with salt and pepper. Transfer
to a serving dish and scatter with
the baby capers (if baby capers are
unavailable, use regular capers,
chopped). Serve with a ploughman's
lunch or as an accompaniment to cold
meat or fish.
Nutritional analysis is not
appropriate for this recipe.

Trim the leeks and wash them thoroughly under cold running water.

Add the leeks to the pan and stir until they are covered with the oil.

Add the vinegar to the cooled leeks and stir to coat.

CHARGRILLED VEGETABLES

Preparation time: 15 minutes +
 40 minutes standing
Total cooking time: 1 hour
Serves 6

2 eggplants
900 g (1¾ lb) orange sweet
 potato
4 zucchini
2 red capsicums
600 g (1¼ lb) button
 mushrooms
1/3 cup (80 ml/2¾ fl oz) olive oil

Basil Dressing
1/2 cup (125 ml/4 fl oz) olive oil
2 cloves garlic, crushed
2 tablespoons balsamic vinegar
1/2 teaspoon sugar
1/3 cup (20 g/¾ oz) fresh basil
 leaves

1 Cut the eggplant into 1 cm (½ inch) thick slices. Place on a wire rack and sprinkle liberally with salt. Leave for 30 minutes, then rinse under cold water and pat dry with paper towels.

2 Cut the sweet potato into 5 mm (¼ inch) slices and the zucchini into 1 cm (½ inch) slices lengthways. Quarter the capsicums, remove the seeds and membranes and chargrill, skin-side-down, until the skin blackens and blisters. (Alternatively, cook the capsicums, skin-side-up, under a preheated grill to blister the skins.) Place in a plastic bag and leave to cool. Peel away the skin.

3 Brush the eggplant, sweet potato, zucchini and mushrooms with oil. Chargrill or barbecue in batches until lightly browned and cooked through.

4 To make the basil dressing, put the oil, garlic, vinegar, sugar and basil in a food processor or blender and process until smooth.

5 Combine the chargrilled vegetables with the basil dressing and mix well. Allow to cool, then cover and refrigerate until ready to use. Return to room temperature before serving.

NUTRITION PER SERVE
Protein 9 g; Fat 20 g; Carbohydrate 28 g; Dietary Fibre 9 g; Cholesterol 0 mg; 1495 kJ (355 cal)

Put the slices of eggplant on a wire rack and sprinkle with salt.

Use a sharp knife to cut the sweet potato into slices.

Once cooled, gently peel the blackened skin off the capsicums.

Brush the vegetables with oil and chargrill or barbecue until lightly browned.

FELAFEL

Preparation time: 30 minutes +
  30 minutes standing + 4 hours soaking
Total cooking time: 25 minutes
Makes 30

2 cups (440 g/14 oz) dried
  chickpeas
1 onion, finely chopped
2 cloves garlic, crushed
2 tablespoons chopped fresh
  parsley
1 tablespoon chopped fresh
  coriander

2 teaspoons ground cumin
1/2 teaspoon baking powder
oil, for deep-frying

1 Soak the chickpeas in 3 cups (750 ml/24 fl oz) of water for 4 hours or overnight. Drain and place in a food processor, and process for 30 seconds, or until finely ground.
2 Add the onion, garlic, parsley, coriander, cumin, baking powder, 1 tablespoon of water, salt and pepper and process for 10 seconds, or until the mixture forms a rough paste. Cover and leave for 30 minutes.
3 Using your hands, shape heaped tablespoons of the felafel mixture into balls and squeeze out any excess liquid. Fill a deep heavy-based pan one third full of oil to 180°C (350°F). and heat until a cube of bread browns in 15 seconds. Gently lower the felafel balls into the oil. Cook in batches of five at a time, for 3–4 minutes each batch. When the balls are well browned, remove with a large slotted spoon. Drain well. Serve with Lebanese bread, tabbouleh and hummus.

NUTRITION PER FELAFEL
Protein 2.5 g; Fat 2.5 g; Carbohydrate 5.5 g; Dietary Fibre 2 g; Cholesterol 0 mg; 193 kJ (45 cal)

Finely grind the chickpeas, then add the remaining ingredients.

Process the ingredients until a rough paste is formed.

With clean hands shape the felafel mixture into balls, squeezing out excess liquid.

Oils & Vinegars

Spice up your marinades, vinaigrettes and dressings with these delicious recipes, or simply enjoy the oil with fresh crusty bread. If you sterilise the storage jar first by rinsing it with boiling water and placing it in a warm oven until it is completely dry, most oils and vinegars will keep for up to 6 months.

TARRAGON VINEGAR

Warm 2 cups (500 ml/16 fl oz) white wine vinegar over low heat. Gently bruise 25 g (³/₄ oz) fresh tarragon leaves in your hands and put in a 2-cup (500 ml/16 fl oz) sterilised wide-necked jar. Pour in the vinegar, seal with a non-metallic lid and shake well. Allow to stand in a warm place for 2 weeks to infuse. Strain and return to the clean sterilised bottle. Add a fresh sprig of tarragon, seal and label. Store in a cool, dark place for up to 6 months. Makes 2 cups (500 ml/16 fl oz).

CHILLI OIL

Place 6 dried chillies and 1 teaspoon chilli powder in a heavy-based pan. Add 3 cups (750 ml/24 fl oz) olive oil, bring to the boil, then lower the heat and simmer for 5 minutes (if it gets too hot the oil will change flavour). Cover with plastic wrap and leave in a cool, dark place for 3 days. Strain the oil into a 3-cup (750 ml/24 fl oz) sterilised bottle. Discard the chillies and add new chillies for decoration. Makes 3 cups (750 ml/24 fl oz). Store in a cool, dark place for up to 6 months.

PARMESAN OIL

Combine 2 cups (500 ml/16 fl oz) olive oil and 100 g (3¹/₂ oz) finely grated Reggiano Parmesan in a small pan. Stir the oil mixture over low heat for 10–15 minutes, or until the Parmesan starts to melt and clump together. Remove from the heat and allow to cool. Strain into a 2-cup (500 ml/16 fl oz) sterilised bottle and add 20 g (³/₄ oz) shaved Parmesan. Seal and label. Store in a cool, dark place for up to 6 months. Makes 2 cups (500 ml/16 fl oz).

INDIAN OIL

Place 1 teaspoon each of garam masala, coriander seeds, cardamom pods and fennel seeds, 3 allspice berries, 3 curry leaves and 1 small dried chilli in a bowl and lightly crush with the back of a spoon. Place in a sterilised bottle with 3 cups (750 ml/24 fl oz) peanut or canola oil. Seal and leave for 3 days in a cool, dark place. Strain into a 3-cup (750 ml/24 fl oz) sterilised bottle. Store in a cool, dark place for up to 3 months. Makes about 3 cups (750 ml/24 fl oz).

SPICY APPLE AND CINNAMON VINEGAR

Combine 2 cups (500 ml/16 fl oz) white wine vinegar, 1/3 cup (30 g/1 oz) finely chopped dried apple slices, 1/4 teaspoon black peppercorns, 2 bay leaves, 1/4 teaspoon yellow mustard seeds, 2 cinnamon sticks, 2 sprigs fresh thyme and 1 peeled garlic clove in a 2-cup (500 ml/16 fl oz) sterilised

From left to right: Tarragon vinegar; Chilli oil; Parmesan oil; Raspberry vinegar; Spicy apple and cinnamon vinegar; Spiced malt vinegar; Indian oil.

jar or bottle. Seal and leave in a cool, dark place for 2 weeks. Strain the vinegar and pour into warm sterilised jars. Store in a cool, dark place for up to 6 months. Makes about 2 cups (500 ml/16 fl oz).

RASPBERRY VINEGAR

Place 2 1/3 cups (290 g/10 oz) fresh or thawed frozen raspberries in a non-metallic bowl and crush gently with the back of a spoon. Over low heat, warm 2 cups (500 ml/16 fl oz) white wine vinegar. Add the vinegar to the raspberries and mix well. Pour into a 2-cup (500 ml/16 fl oz) sterilised jar and keep in a warm place for 2 weeks, shaking regularly. Strain through a muslin-lined sieve into a small pan. Add 2 teapoons caster sugar and stir over medium heat until the sugar has dissolved. Pour into a warm sterilised

jar or bottle. Add 2–3 raspberries, if desired, seal and label. Store in a cool, dark place for up to 6 months. Makes about 2 cups (500 ml/16 fl oz).

SPICED MALT VINEGAR

Place 2 cups (500 ml/16 fl oz) malt vinegar in a pan. Add a 1 cm piece (10 g) fresh ginger cut into four pieces. Add 1 cinnamon stick, 2 teaspoons allspice berries, 1/2 teaspoon black peppercorns, 1 teaspoon brown mustard seeds, 10 cloves and warm over low heat. Pour into a warm, sterilised, 2-cup (500 ml/16 fl oz) wide-necked jar and seal with a non-metallic lid. Stand in a warm place for 2 weeks. Put some peppercorns into a sterilised 2-cup (500 ml/16 fl oz) bottle. Strain and pour the vinegar into the bottle. Seal and store in a cool, dark place for up to 6 months. Makes 2 cups (500 ml/16 fl oz).

HERB-FILLED RAVIOLI

Preparation time: 1 hour + 30 minutes
  standing
Total cooking time: 10 minutes
Serves 4

300 g (10 oz) plain flour
3 eggs, beaten
3 tablespoons oil
1 cup (250 g/8 oz) ricotta
2 tablespoons grated Parmesan
2 teaspoons chopped fresh
  chives
1 tablespoon chopped flat-leaf
  parsley
2 teaspoons chopped fresh basil
1 teaspoon chopped fresh lemon
  thyme or thyme
1 egg, beaten, extra

1 Sift the flour into a bowl and make a well in the centre. Gradually mix in the eggs and oil. Turn out onto a lightly floured surface and knead for 6 minutes, or until smooth. Cover with plastic wrap and leave for 30 minutes.
2 To make the filling, mix the ricotta, Parmesan and herbs. Season well.
3 Divide the dough into four portions and shape each into a log. Keeping the unworked portions covered, take one portion and flatten it with one or two rolls of a rolling pin. With machine rollers set to the widest setting, crank the dough through two or three times. Fold it into thirds, turn the dough by 90 degrees and feed it through again. If the dough feels sticky, flour it lightly each time it is rolled. Repeat the rolling and folding 8–10 times until the dough feels smooth and elastic. Reduce the width of the rollers by one setting and pass the dough through without folding it. Repeat, setting the rollers one notch closer each time until you have reached a thickness of 2 mm (1/6 inch). Roll another sheet slightly larger than the first and cover with a tea towel.
4 Spread the smaller sheet out onto a work surface. Spoon 1 teaspoon of the filling at 5 cm (2 inch) intervals. Brush the beaten egg between the filling along the cutting lines. Place the larger sheet on top. Press the two sheets together along the cutting line.

Cut the ravioli with a pastry wheel or knife. Transfer to a lightly floured baking tray. Repeat with the remaining dough and filling. Can be stored in the refrigerator for 1–2 days.
5 Cook the ravioli in a large pan of salted boiling water for 5–8 minutes and top with a sauce of your choice.

NUTRITION PER SERVE
Protein 25 g; Fat 30 g; Carbohydrate 55 g; Dietary Fibre 3 g; Cholesterol 215 mg; 2395 kJ (570 cal)

Mix together the ricotta, Parmesan and herbs and season with salt and pepper.

Brush the beaten egg between the filling along the cutting lines.

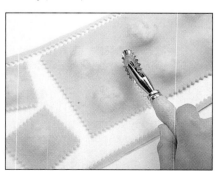
Press the two sheets of dough together and cut the ravioli with a pastry wheel.

SEMI-DRIED TOMATOES

Preparation time: 10 minutes +
  24 hours refrigeration
Total cooking time: 2 hours 30 minutes
Fills a 500 ml (16 fl oz) jar

16 Roma tomatoes
3 tablespoons fresh thyme,
  chopped
2 tablespoons olive oil

1 Preheat the oven to warm 160°C (315°F/Gas 2–3). Cut the tomatoes into quarters lengthways and lay them skin-side-down on a wire rack in a baking tray.
2 Sprinkle with 1 teaspoon of salt, 1 teaspoon of cracked black pepper and the thyme and cook in the oven for 2½ hours. Check occasionally to make sure the tomatoes don't burn.
3 Toss the tomatoes in the olive oil and leave to cool before packing into

sterilised jars and sealing. Store in the refrigerator for 24 hours before using. Semi-dried tomatoes should be eaten within 3–4 days.

Nutritional analysis is not appropriate for this recipe.

COOK'S FILE

Note: To sterilise a storage jar, rinse with boiling water then place in a warm oven until completely dry. Do not dry with a tea towel.

Cut the tomatoes into quarters and lay them skin-side-down on a wire rack.

Season the tomatoes with salt, cracked pepper and fresh thyme.

Cover the tomatoes with olive oil and toss until well coated.

47

SWEET CHILLI CHICKEN

Preparation time: 15 minutes +
  2 hours refrigeration
Total cooking time: 20 minutes
Serves 6

1 kg (2 lb) chicken thigh fillets
2 tablespoons lime juice
1/2 cup (125 ml/4 fl oz) sweet
  chilli sauce
3 tablespoons kecap manis
  (see Note)

1 Trim any excess fat from the chicken thigh fillets and cut them in half. Transfer to a shallow non-metallic dish.
2 Place the lime juice, sweet chilli sauce and kecap manis in a bowl and whisk to combine.
3 Pour the marinade over the chicken, cover and refrigerate for 2 hours.
4 Chargrill or bake in a preheated moderately hot 200°C (400°F/Gas 6) oven for 20 minutes, or until the chicken is tender and cooked through and the marinade has caramelised.

NUTRITION PER SERVE
Protein 35 g; Fat 4.5 g; Carbohydrate 4 g; Dietary Fibre 1 g; Cholesterol 85 mg; 880 kJ (210 cal)

COOK'S FILE

Note: Kecap manis (ketjap manis) is a thick Indonesian sauce, similar to—but sweeter than—soy sauce, and is generally flavoured with garlic and star anise. Store in a cool, dry place and refrigerate after opening. If not available, use soy sauce sweetened with a little soft brown sugar.

Trim the excess fat from the thigh fillets, and cut them in half.

To make the marinade, whisk together the lime juice, sweet chilli sauce and kecap manis.

Pour the marinade over the chicken, then cover and refrigerate.

Carefully peel the ginger, then cut it into thin slices.

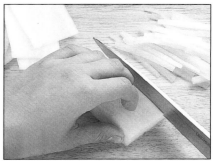

Use a sharp knife to cut the daikon or white radish into julienne strips.

Mix together the vinegar, sugar and ginger and stir until the sugar has dissolved.

Once the vinegar syrup has cooled, pour it over the vegetables.

PICKLED DAIKON WITH CARROT AND GINGER

Preparation time: 25 minutes +
  1–2 days marinating
Total cooking time: 5 minutes
Serves 8

2 cups (500 ml/16 fl oz) white
    vinegar
2 cups (500 g/1 lb) sugar
50 g (1¾ oz) fresh ginger,
    finely sliced
1 daikon (about 500 g/1 lb) or
    white radish, julienned
4 carrots, julienned

1 Put the vinegar, sugar and 3 slices of ginger in a pan. Stir over medium heat to dissolve the sugar. Bring to the boil, then remove the pan from the heat and allow the mixture to cool to room temperature.

2 Place the daikon or radish, carrot and remaining ginger in a bowl and mix together well.

3 Pour the vinegar syrup over the vegetables. Transfer the vegetables and syrup to sterilised jars and seal. Turn the jars upside down for 2 minutes, then invert and allow to cool. Label and date, then leave to marinate in a cool place for 1–2 days before eating.

NUTRITION PER SERVE
Protein 1 g; Fat 0.5 g; Carbohydrate 65 g; Dietary Fibre 2 g; Cholesterol 0 mg; 1125 kJ (270 cal)

COOK'S FILE

Note: To sterilise a storage jar, rinse with boiling water then place in a warm oven until completely dry. Do not dry with a tea towel.
Serving suggestion: The pickle can be eaten as a side salad with Asian meals or used in stir-fries.

Storage time: Refrigerate after opening. Once opened, the pickle will keep for up to 3 months in the refrigerator.

CORNISH PASTIES

Preparation time: 35 minutes +
  30 minutes refrigeration
Total cooking time: 45 minutes
Makes 6 pasties

2½ cups (310 g/10 oz) plain
  flour
125 g (4 oz) butter, chilled and
  chopped
160 g (5½ oz) round steak,
  finely chopped
1 small potato, finely chopped
1 small onion, finely chopped
1 small carrot, finely chopped
1–2 teaspoons Worcestershire
  sauce
2 tablespoons beef stock
1 egg, lightly beaten

1 Grease a baking tray. Place the flour, butter and a pinch of salt in a food processor and process for 15 seconds, or until crumbly. Add 4–5 tablespoons of water and process in short bursts until the mixture comes together (add more water if needed). Turn out onto a floured surface and form into a ball. Cover with plastic wrap and chill for 30 minutes. Preheat the oven to hot 210°C (415°F/Gas 6–7).
2 Mix together the steak, potato, onion, carrot, Worcestershire sauce and stock. Season well.
3 Divide the dough into six portions. Roll out each portion to 3 mm (1/8 inch) thick. Using a 16 cm (6½ inch) diameter plate as a guide, cut out 6 circles. Divide the filling evenly and put in the centre of each pastry circle.
4 Brush the edges with beaten egg and form into a semi-circle. Pinch the edges to form a frill and place on the tray. Brush with the remaining beaten egg and bake for 15 minutes. Lower the heat to moderate 180°C (350°F/Gas 4). Cook for 25–30 minutes, or until golden.

NUTRITION PER PASTY
Protein 15 g; Fat 20 g; Carbohydrate 40 g; Dietary Fibre 3 g; Cholesterol 100 mg; 1665 kJ (395 cal)

Process the flour, butter and salt until the mixture resembles fine breadcrumbs.

Mix together the steak, potato, onion, carrot, Worcestershire sauce and stock.

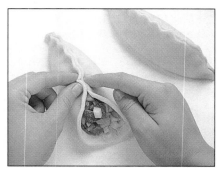

Fold the pastry over the filling to form a semi-circle and pinch to close.

CAPERS IN BALSAMIC VINEGAR

Preparation time: 5 minutes
Total cooking time: 45 minutes
Fills a 250 ml (8 fl oz) jar

2 tablespoons olive oil
1 red onion, finely chopped
1 clove garlic, crushed
2 teaspoons soft brown sugar

170 g (5½ oz) capers, rinsed and drained
⅓ cup (80 ml/2¾ fl oz) balsamic vinegar

1 Heat the oil in a pan, add the onion and fry over low heat for 15 minutes, or until translucent. Add the garlic and fry for 1 minute. Increase the heat and cook the onion and garlic for 5 minutes, or until it starts to brown. Add the sugar and cook for 15 minutes, or until the onion is caramelised.

2 Add the capers and vinegar. Bring to the boil, then reduce the heat and simmer until the liquid is syrupy. Rinse a glass jar with boiling water and dry in a warm oven. Spoon in the capers and liquid and seal. Store for up to 3 months. Refrigerate after opening.

NUTRITION PER TABLESPOON
Protein 0.5 g; Fat 3 g; Carbohydrate 1.5 g; Dietary Fibre 0 g; Cholesterol 0 mg; 145 kJ (35 cal)

Rinse the capers under cold water and drain well.

Add the brown sugar to the onion and garlic and stir over heat until caramelised.

Stir the capers and balsamic vinegar into the onion mixture and bring to the boil.

PORK AND VEAL TERRINE

Preparation time: 20 minutes +
  overnight refrigeration
Total cooking time: 1 hour 20 minutes
Serves 6

8–10 thin slices rindless bacon
1 tablespoon olive oil
1 onion, chopped
2 cloves garlic, crushed
1 kg (2 lb) pork and veal mince
1 cup (80 g/2¾ oz) fresh
  breadcrumbs
1 egg, beaten
¼ cup (60 ml/2 fl oz) brandy
3 teaspoons chopped fresh
  thyme
¼ cup (15 g/½ oz) chopped
  fresh parsley

1 Preheat the oven to moderate 180°C (350°F/Gas 4). Lightly grease a 25 x 11 cm (10 x 4½ inch) terrine. Line the terrine with the bacon so that it hangs over the sides.
2 Heat the oil in a frying pan, add the onion and garlic and cook for 2–3 minutes, or until the onion is soft. Mix the onion with the mince, breadcrumbs, egg, brandy, thyme and parsley in a large bowl. Season with salt and pepper. Fry a small piece of the mixture to check the seasoning, and adjust if necessary.
3 Spoon the mixture into the bacon-lined terrine, pressing down firmly. Fold the bacon over the top of the terrine, cover with foil and place in a baking dish.
4 Place enough cold water in the baking dish to come half way up the side of the terrine. Bake for 1–1¼ hours, or until the juices run clear when the terrine is pierced with a skewer. Remove the terrine from the water-filled baking dish and pour off the excess juices. Cover with foil, then put a piece of heavy cardboard, cut to fit, on top of the terrine. Put weights or food cans on top of the cardboard to compress the terrine. Refrigerate overnight, then cut into slices to serve.

NUTRITION PER SERVE
Protein 15 g; Fat 7.5 g; Carbohydrate 10 g; Dietary Fibre 1 g; Cholesterol 60 mg; 800 kJ (190 cal)

COOK'S FILE

Storage time: The terrine can be made ahead of time and stored, covered, in the refrigerator for up to 5 days.

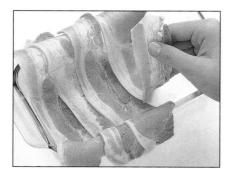

Line the terrine dish with the bacon strips so that they drape over the sides.

Mix together the onion mixture, mince, breadcrumbs, egg, brandy and herbs.

Press the mixture firmly into the terrine dish and fold the bacon over the top.

HARISSA

Preparation time: 30 minutes +
    1 hour soaking
Total cooking time: Nil
Fills a 600 ml (20 fl oz) jar

125 g (4 oz) dried red chillies
1 tablespoon dried mint
1 tablespoon ground coriander
1 tablespoon ground cumin
1 teaspoon ground caraway seeds
10 cloves garlic, chopped
1/2 cup (125 ml/4 fl oz) olive oil

1 Remove the stems from the chillies, roughly chop, then cover with boiling water and soak for 1 hour. Drain and place in a food processor. Add the mint, spices, garlic, 1/2 teaspoon salt and 1 tablespoon of oil. Process for 20 seconds, then scrape down the side of the bowl. Process for a further 30 seconds. Add 2 tablespoons of oil and process again; repeat and process until a thick paste forms.

2 Spoon the paste into a sterilised jar, cover with a thin layer of olive oil and seal. Label and date. Keep in the refrigerator for up to 6 months.

NUTRITION PER TABLESPOON
Protein 0 g; Fat 4 g; Carbohydrate 0.5 g; Dietary Fibre 0.5 g; Cholesterol 0 mg; 160 kJ (40 cal)

COOK'S FILE

Note: To sterilise a storage jar, rinse with boiling water then place in a warm oven until completely dry. Do not dry with a tea towel.

Serving suggestion: Delicious served with tagines and couscous. Alternatively, try adding it to your salad dressings, marinades and pasta sauces to give them an extra kick.

Wearing rubber gloves to protect your hands, remove the stems and roughly chop the chillies.

Process the chillies, mint, spices, garlic, salt and oil and scrape down the side of the bowl.

Spoon the paste into a sterilised jar and top with a thin layer of olive oil.

POTATO GNOCCHI

Preparation time: 30 minutes
Total cooking time: 1 hour 5 minutes
Serves 6

1 kg (2 lb) floury potatoes, unpeeled
1 egg yolk
3/4 cup (90 g/3 oz) plain flour

1 Preheat the oven to moderately hot 200°C (400°F/Gas 6). Prick the unpeeled potatoes with a fork and bake for 1 hour, or until tender. Don't wrap them in foil. When cool enough to handle but still hot, peel and mash with a masher. Push through a fine sieve or process through a food mill into a bowl and make a well in the centre. Add the egg yolk, three-quarters of the flour and 1/2 teaspoon of salt and gradually work it in with your hands. When a loose dough forms, transfer to a lightly floured surface and knead gently with lightly floured hands. Work in the remaining flour. (If the dough is too sticky you may need to add more flour.)

2 Divide the mixture into eight portions. Roll each piece into a 20 cm (8 inch) rope. Cut the rope into 1 cm (1/2 inch) pieces with a floured knife. Put a piece of dough on the prongs of a fork and press down with your finger, rolling the dough as you do so. Continue with the remaining pieces. Place in a single layer on a tray lightly dusted with flour.

3 Cook the gnocchi in a large pan of boiling water for 2–3 minutes, or until they rise to the surface. Top with a sauce (see page 76) and grated Parmesan.

NUTRITION PER SERVE
Protein 6 g; Fat 1 g; Carbohydrate 35 g; Dietary Fibre 3 g; Cholesterol 30 mg; 715 kJ (170 cal)

COOK'S FILE

Storage time: Gnocchi can be frozen for up to 2 months and do not need to be thawed, but note that the cooking time will increase to 4–5 minutes.

Using a wooden spoon, push the mashed potatoes through a fine sieve.

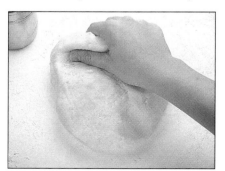

Transfer the dough to a lightly floured surface and knead gently.

Put the dough on a fork, press down with your finger and roll the gnocchi.

Use a sharp knife to chop the tarragon leaves into small pieces.

Cover the base of the tin with chives and top with the cream cheese mixture.

Use a palette knife to spread the cream cheese mixture evenly into the tin.

Starting from the longest edge, roll the cream cheese and herbs into a log.

HERB CHEESE LOG

Preparation time: 25 minutes +
  3 hours refrigeration
Total cooking time: Nil
Serves 6

500 g (1 lb) cream cheese,
  at room temperature
1 tablespoon lemon juice
1 clove garlic, crushed
2 teaspoons chopped fresh
  thyme
2 teaspoons chopped fresh
  tarragon
1 tablespoon chopped fresh
  flat-leaf parsley
1 cup (50 g/1²/₃ oz) chopped
  fresh chives

1 Put the cream cheese in a large bowl and beat with electric beaters until soft and creamy. Mix in the lemon juice and garlic. Mix together the thyme, tarragon and parsley.

2 Line a 20 x 30 cm (8 x 12 inch) tin with foil. Spread the chives over the base, then spoon the cream cheese mixture over the chives. Using a palette knife, gently spread the mixture into the tin, pushing it into any gaps. Sprinkle the combined herbs evenly over the cheese.

3 Lift the foil from the tin and place on a work surface. Roll into a log, starting from the longest edge, peeling back the foil as you go. Cover and place on a baking tray. Refrigerate for at least 3 hours, or preferably overnight. Serve with water crackers or fresh crusty bread.

NUTRITION PER SERVE
Protein 7 g; Fat 28 g; Carbohydrate 2.5 g; Dietary Fibre 0.5 g; Cholesterol 80 mg; 1188 kJ (285 cal)

COOK'S FILE

Variation: Make a roulade by rolling into a log from the shortest edge.

Pestos & Tapenades

Cheer up seafood and chicken, spice up vegetables and soups, stir through pasta, or simply serve as a dip. Keep a jar of pesto or tapenade handy and you can cope with any catering emergency—just make sure the jar is sterilised first by rinsing it with boiling water and drying it in a warm oven.

TRADITIONAL PESTO

Combine 2 cups (60 g/2 oz) lightly packed fresh basil leaves, $1/4$ cup (40 g/$1^1/4$ oz) lightly toasted pine nuts, 2 coarsely chopped large cloves of garlic and a pinch of salt in a food processor or blender. Process until finely minced. With the motor running, slowly pour in $1/3$ cup (80 ml/$2^3/4$ fl oz) extra virgin olive oil. Add $1/2$ cup (50 g/$1^3/4$ oz) freshly grated Parmesan and freshly ground black pepper and process until just combined. Transfer to a sterilised jar and cover the surface with a thin layer of extra virgin olive oil. Seal and refrigerate for up to 7 days. Serve as a pasta sauce, with chicken and shellfish, as a dressing for vegetables or as a dip. Makes about 1 cup (250 g/8 oz).

RED PESTO

Put a 200 g ($6^1/2$ oz) jar sun-dried tomatoes in oil, $1/3$ cup (10 g/$1/4$ oz) fresh basil leaves, $1/3$ cup (7 g/$1/4$ oz) fresh flat-leaf parsley leaves, 2 chopped cloves garlic, 2 teaspoons rinsed and drained capers, 1 large anchovy fillet and 4 tablespoons lightly toasted pine nuts in a food processor or blender. Process until finely minced. With the motor running, pour in 2 tablespoons red wine vinegar and $1/2$ cup (125 ml/4 fl oz) extra virgin olive oil. When blended, add 2 tablespoons freshly grated Parmesan and freshly ground black pepper. Transfer to a sterilised jar and cover the surface with a thin coating of extra virgin olive oil. Seal and refrigerate for up to 2 weeks. Serve as a pasta sauce if thinned with a little more olive oil, as a dip for crudités or with white-fleshed fish. Makes about $1^1/4$ cups (310 g/10 oz).

From left to right: Traditional pesto; Red pesto; Rocket and pecan pesto; Traditional olive tapenade; North African tapenade.

ROCKET AND PECAN PESTO

Place 1²/₃ cups (60 g/2 oz) young rocket leaves, ¹/₃ cup (7 g/¹/₄ oz) flat-leaf parsley, 12 large pecan halves and 2 coarsely chopped large cloves garlic in a food processor or blender. Process until the ingredients are well combined and finely minced. With the motor running, slowly pour in ¹/₂ cup (125 ml/4 fl oz) extra virgin olive oil. Add ¹/₃ cup (35 g/1¹/₄ oz) freshly grated Parmesan and process until well combined. Lightly season to taste with salt. Transfer the pesto to a sterilised jar and cover the surface with a thin coating of extra virgin olive oil. Seal and refrigerate for up to 7 days. Serve as a dip with crudités and crusty bread, as a pasta sauce or drizzled over chicken. Makes about ³/₄ cup (185 g/6 oz).
Variation: For a delicious alternative, try replacing the pecans with golden walnut halves.

TRADITIONAL OLIVE TAPENADE

Place 1 tablespoon rinsed and drained capers, 30 g (1 oz) drained anchovy fillets, 50 g (1³/₄ oz) drained tuna in oil, 1 small clove garlic, 1 cup (125 g/4 oz) sliced pitted black olives and 2 tablespoons lemon juice in a food processor or blender. Process until finely chopped. While the motor is still running, add 2 tablespoons extra virgin olive oil and 1¹/₂ tablespoons cognac, if you wish. Season to taste with black pepper. Transfer to a sterilised jar. Seal and refrigerate for up to 2 weeks. Serve as a spread for bread and crudités or as a sauce for tuna and fish steaks. Makes about 1¹/₄ cups (310 g/10 oz).
Variation: For a slightly different flavour, replace the black olives with good-quality green olives.

NORTH AFRICAN TAPENADE

Put a pinch of saffron in a small bowl with 1 teaspoon hot water and set aside. Put ²/₃ cup (140 g/4¹/₂ oz) pitted green olives, 3 anchovy fillets, ¹/₄ teaspoon dried oregano, 2 tablespoons toasted pine nuts, 1 chopped clove garlic and ¹/₈ teaspoon ground cumin in a food processor or blender. Process until finely minced. With the motor running, add 3 teaspoons lime juice, 3 tablespoons extra virgin olive oil and the saffron and water mixture. Stop processing as soon as the ingredients are blended, and transfer to a sterilised jar. Seal and store in the refrigerator for up to 2 weeks. Delicious served with seafood, particularly tuna, as a pasta sauce when thinned with a little more olive oil, or on bruschetta. Makes about 1 cup (250 g/8 oz).

RATATOUILLE TARTS

Preparation time: 40 minutes +
  15 minutes refrigeration +
  20 minutes standing
Total cooking time: 1 hour 10 minutes
Makes 12

3 cups (375 g/12 oz) plain
  flour
170 g (5½ oz) butter, chilled
  and chopped

Ratatouille Filling
1 eggplant (about 500 g)
¼ cup (60 ml/2 fl oz) oil
1 onion, chopped
2 cloves garlic, crushed
2 zucchini, sliced
1 red capsicum, chopped
1 green capsicum, chopped
250 g (8 oz) cherry tomatoes,
  halved
1 tablespoon balsamic vinegar
1 cup (125 g/4 oz) grated
  Cheddar

1 Sift the flour into a bowl and add the butter. Using your fingertips, rub the butter into the flour until the mixture resembles fine breadcrumbs. Make a well in the centre and add ½ cup (125 ml/4 fl oz) chilled water. Mix together with a flat-bladed knife, adding a little more water if necessary, until the dough just comes together.
2 Gather the dough into a ball and divide into 12 portions. Grease 12 loose-based fluted flan tins measuring 8 cm (3 inches) across the base and 3 cm (1¼ inches) deep. Roll each portion of dough out on a sheet of non-stick baking paper to a circle a little larger than the tins. Lift the pastry into the tins and press well

into the sides, then trim away any excess pastry. Refrigerate for 15 minutes. Preheat the oven to moderately hot 200°C (400°F/Gas 6).
3 Put all the tins on baking trays, prick the pastry bases all over with a fork and bake for 20–25 minutes, or until the pastry is fully cooked and lightly golden. Cool completely.
4 Meanwhile, to make the ratatouille filling, cut the eggplant into 2 cm (¾ inch) cubes, put into a colander and sprinkle generously with salt. Leave for 20 minutes, then rinse, drain and pat dry with paper towels.
5 Heat 2 tablespoons of the oil in a large frying pan. Cook the eggplant for 8–10 minutes, or until browned. Drain on paper towels. Heat the remaining oil and add the onion. Cook over medium heat for 5 minutes, or until very soft. Add the garlic and cook for 1 minute, then add the zucchini and capsicum and cook, stirring frequently, for 10 minutes, or until softened. Add the eggplant and tomatoes. Cook, stirring, for 2 minutes. Transfer to a bowl, stir in the vinegar, then cover and cool completely.
6 Preheat the oven to moderate 180°C (350°F/Gas 4). Divide the mixture among the tart shells with a slotted spoon, draining off any excess liquid. Sprinkle with the Cheddar and cook for 10–15 minutes, or until the cheese has melted and the tarts are warmed through.

NUTRITION PER TART
Protein 7.5 g; Fat 20 g; Carbohydrate 25 g; Dietary Fibre 3.5 g; Cholesterol 45 mg; 1328 kJ (317 cal)

COOK'S FILE

Note: The ratatouille filling can be made a day ahead and stored in an airtight container in the refrigerator.

Rub the butter into the sifted flour until the mixture resembles fine breadcrumbs.

Press the pastry well into the side of the tin and cut away any excess.

Prick the pastry bases with a fork to reduce puffiness.

Sprinkle a generous amount of salt on the eggplant cubes.

Add the eggplant and tomatoes, then cook, stirring, for 2 minutes.

Pour the balsamic vinegar over the vegetables and mix well.

VEGETABLE SAMOSAS

Preparation time: 35 minutes +
  20 minutes refrigeration
Total cooking time: 30 minutes
Makes 32

4 cups (500 g/1 lb) plain flour
2 tablespoons oil

Vegetable Filling
600 g (1¼ lb) waxy potatoes
185 g (6 oz) cauliflower florets,
  chopped
2 tablespoons vegetable oil
1 onion, chopped
2 cloves garlic, finely chopped
2 tablespoons grated fresh
  ginger
2 tablespoons mild curry
  powder
²/3 cup (100 g/3½ oz) frozen
  peas
2 tablespoons lemon juice
oil, for deep-frying

1 In a food processor, process the flour and 1 teaspoon of salt for 5 seconds. Add the combined oil and 1 cup (250 ml/8 fl oz) of warm water. Process in short bursts until the mixture just comes together. Turn out onto a floured surface and gather into a ball. Cover with plastic wrap and refrigerate for 20 minutes.
2 To make the vegetable filling, chop the potatoes into quarters and cook until tender, then cool and finely dice. Boil or steam the cauliflower until tender, cool and finely dice. Heat the oil in a large frying pan and cook the onion over medium heat for 5 minutes, or until soft. Add the garlic, ginger and curry powder and cook for 2 minutes. Add the potato, cauliflower,

peas and lemon juice and mix well. Remove from the heat and cool.
3 Divide the dough into 16 portions. On a lightly floured surface, roll each portion into a 15 cm (6 inch) round, cut the rounds in half and put a tablespoon of the mixture in the middle of each semi-circle. Brush the edge with a little water and fold the pastry over the mixture, pressing the edges to seal.

4 Fill a wok or deep pan one third full of oil and heat until a cube of bread browns in 15 seconds. Deep-fry the samosas in batches for 1 minute, or until golden. Drain on paper towels and serve hot with mango chutney, sweet chilli sauce or yoghurt.

NUTRITION PER SAMOSA
Protein 2.5 g; Fat 3.5 g; Carbohydrate 15 g; Dietary Fibre 1.5 g; Cholesterol 0 mg; 410 kJ (95 cal)

Process the flour, salt, oil and water until the mixture just comes together.

Add the potato, cauliflower, peas and lemon juice to the onion mixture.

Brush the edge of the dough with water, then fold over the filling and seal.

Strain the liquid through a fine sieve and leave to cool.

When cool enough to handle, pull the chicken flesh off the bones.

Process the chicken flesh with the butter and spices until smooth.

Pour the yellow clarified butter over the potted chicken.

POTTED CHICKEN

Preparation time: 15 minutes
  + 2 hours refrigeration
Total cooking time: 1 hour
Serves 6

6 chicken thighs, skin removed
1 onion, sliced
1 carrot, sliced
6 peppercorns
1 bay leaf
pinch of ground mace
pinch of cayenne pepper
1/4 teaspoon freshly grated
  nutmeg
200 g (6½ oz) unsalted butter,
  softened

1 Place the chicken thighs, onion, carrot, peppercorns and bay leaf in a pan and add 2 cups (500 ml/16 fl oz) of water. Bring to the boil, skimming off any foam. Reduce the heat, then cover and simmer for 30 minutes, or until tender and cooked through.

2 Remove the chicken, then rapidly boil the remaining liquid until it has reduced to about 1/4 cup (60 ml/ 2 fl oz). Strain through a fine sieve and allow to cool.

3 Remove the chicken flesh from the bones. Place the flesh in a food processor with the liquid and process until smooth. Add the mace, cayenne pepper, nutmeg and 150 g (5 oz) of the butter. Season to taste with salt and pepper and process until combined and smooth.

4 Put the chicken mixture in a 3-cup (750 ml/24 fl oz) ceramic dish. Melt the remaining butter in a small pan and pour the yellow clarified butter onto the surface of the chicken, leaving the white milk solids in the pan. Refrigerate for 2 hours, or until the butter sets.

NUTRITION PER SERVE
Protein 25 g; Fat 30 g; Carbohydrate 1.5 g; Dietary Fibre 0.5 g; Cholesterol 140 mg; 1590 kJ (380 cal)

CORN MUFFINS

Preparation time: 20 minutes
Total cooking time: 25 minutes
Makes 12

2¹/2 cups (310 g/10 oz) self-
   raising flour
¹/2 cup (75 g/2¹/2 oz) cornmeal
1 cup (250 ml/8 fl oz) milk
125 g (4 oz) butter, melted
2 eggs, lightly beaten
130 g (4¹/2 oz) can corn kernels,
   drained
2 spring onions, finely chopped
¹/2 cup (60 g/2 oz) grated
   Cheddar

1 Preheat the oven to hot 210°C (415°F/Gas 6–7). Grease two trays of six ¹/2-cup (125 ml/4 fl oz) muffin holes with butter. Sift the flour and cornmeal into a large bowl and make a well in the centre.
2 Whisk together the milk, butter, eggs, corn, spring onion, Cheddar and salt and pepper in a separate bowl and pour into the well. Fold gently with a metal spoon until all the ingredients are just combined. Do not overmix—the mixture should still be very lumpy.
3 Spoon the mixture into the tin and bake for 20–25 minutes, or until lightly golden. Leave for 5 minutes before removing from the tin. Serve split in half spread with butter or cream cheese. Delicious warm or at room temperature.

NUTRITION PER MUFFIN
Protein 6 g; Fat 12 g; Carbohydrate 27 g; Dietary Fibre 1.5 g; Cholesterol 65 mg; 1009 kJ (240 cal)

COOK'S FILE

Variation: Muffins are so versatile, you can virtually add whatever you have in the cupboard. Try adding 2 tablespoons chopped chives, 1/4 cup (40 g/1¹/4 oz) chopped, drained sundried tomatoes or capsicum in oil, 2 finely chopped rashers of bacon, 2 finely chopped red chillies or ¹/2 finely chopped red or green capsicum into the mixture with the milk and Cheddar. Another delicious variation is to sprinkle sesame or sunflower seeds over the muffins just before baking.

Using a sharp knife, finely chop the spring onions.

Sift the flour and cornmeal into a large bowl and make a well in the centre.

Pour in the milk mixture and fold gently until just combined.

Spoon the dough into the muffin holes and bake until lightly golden.

CHEESE STICKS

Preparation time: 20 minutes +
20 minutes refrigeration
Total cooking time: 10 minutes
Makes 30

1¼ cups (155 g/5 oz) plain flour
100 g (3½ oz) unsalted butter,
  chilled and chopped
¾ cup (100 g/3½ oz) grated
  Gruyère
1 tablespoon finely chopped
  fresh oregano
1 egg yolk
1 tablespoon sea salt flakes

1 Line two baking trays with baking paper. Put the flour and butter in a food processor and process in short bursts until the mixture resembles fine breadcrumbs. Add the Gruyère and oregano and process for 5–10 seconds, or until just combined. Add the egg yolk and about 1 tablespoon water, and process until the dough just comes together.
2 Turn out onto a lightly floured surface and gather into a ball. Form two teaspoons of dough into a ball and then roll out into a stick about 12 cm (5 inches) long and place on the baking trays. Repeat with the remaining dough, then cover with plastic wrap and refrigerate for 15–20 minutes. Preheat the oven to moderately hot 200°C (400°F/Gas 6).
3 Lightly brush the sticks with water and sprinkle with the sea salt flakes. Bake for 10 minutes, or until golden. Cool on a wire rack and serve with dips or as part of an antipasto platter.

NUTRITION PER STICK
Protein 2 g; Fat 4 g; Carbohydrate 4 g; Dietary Fibre 0.5 g; Cholesterol 18 mg; 250 kJ (60 cal)

COOK'S FILE

Storage time: Cheese sticks will keep for up to 1 week in an airtight container.

Add the egg yolk and a little water and process until the dough clumps together.

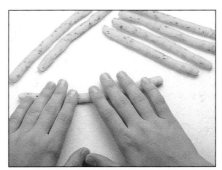

Roll the balls of dough into sticks about 12 cm (5 inches) long.

Brush the sticks with water and sprinkle with sea salt flakes before baking.

MARINATED FETA

Preparation time: 10 minutes +
  1 week refrigeration
Total cooking time: Nil
Serves 6 (as part of an antipasto platter)

350 g (11 oz) feta
1 tablespoon dried oregano
1 teaspoon coriander seeds
1 tablespoon cracked black
  pepper
125 g (4 oz) sun-dried
  tomatoes in oil
4 small fresh red chillies
3–4 sprigs fresh rosemary
olive oil

1 Pat the feta dry with paper towels, and cut into 2 cm (3/4 inch) cubes. Place in a bowl and sprinkle the oregano, coriander seeds and pepper over the cheese.
2 Drain the sun-dried tomatoes over a bowl so that you retain all of the oil. Arrange the feta, chillies, rosemary and sun-dried tomatoes in a sterilised 3-cup (750 ml/24 fl oz) wide-necked jar with a clip-top lid. Cover with the reserved sun-dried tomato oil— you should have about 1/4 cup (60 ml/ 2 fl oz)—and top up with olive oil. Seal and refrigerate for 1 week. Serve at room temperature.

NUTRITION PER SERVE
Protein 10 g; Fat 15 g; Carbohydrate 1 g; Dietary Fibre 0.5 g; Cholesterol 40 mg; 698 kJ (167 cal)

COOK'S FILE

Note: To sterilise a storage jar, rinse with boiling water then place in a warm oven until completely dry.
Storage time: Marinated feta will keep in the refrigerator for 1–2 months.

Sprinkle the oregano, coriander seeds and pepper over the cubes of feta.

Drain the sun-dried tomatoes over a small bowl to retain the oil.

Arrange the ingredients in the jar and pour in the sun-dried tomato oil.

GARLIC AND HERB MARINATED ARTICHOKES

Preparation time: 20 minutes + overnight refrigeration
Total cooking time: Nil
Serves 8 (as part of an antipasto platter)

2 cloves garlic, chopped
1/2 cup (125 ml/4 fl oz) olive oil
2 tablespoons finely chopped fresh dill
1/4 cup (15 g/1/2 oz) finely chopped fresh parsley
2 tablespoons finely chopped fresh basil
2 tablespoons lemon juice
2 x 400 g (13 oz) canned artichokes
1/4 cup (40 g/11/4 oz) finely diced red capsicum

1 To make the marinade, whisk together the garlic, oil, herbs and lemon juice in a bowl. Season with salt and cracked black pepper.

2 Drain the artichokes and add to the bowl with the capsicum. Mix well to coat. Cover and marinate in the refrigerator overnight. Serve as part of an antipasto platter or use in salads.

NUTRITION PER SERVE
Protein 1 g; Fat 7.5 g; Carbohydrate 1 g; Dietary Fibre 1.5 g; Cholesterol 0 mg; 320 kJ (75 cal)

COOK'S FILE

Storage time: The artichokes will keep in an airtight container in the refrigerator for up to 1 week.

Use a sharp knife to finely chop the fresh dill.

Combine the garlic, oil, herbs and lemon juice to make the marinade.

Drain the artichokes well before adding to the marinade.

BEEF AND MUSHROOM LASAGNE

Preparation time: 30 minutes
Total cooking time: 2 hours
Serves 8

1 tablespoon olive oil
2 cloves garlic, crushed
1 onion, chopped
1 carrot, grated
1 stick celery, diced
125 g (4 oz) mushrooms,
    chopped
600 g (1¼ lb) minced beef
2½ cups (600 ml/20 fl oz)
    Italian tomato passata
1 teaspoon dried oregano leaves
300 g (10 oz) instant lasagne
    sheets
1 cup (100 g/3½ oz) grated
    Parmesan

Cheese Sauce
60 g (2 oz) butter
⅓ cup (40 g/1¼ oz) plain flour
1 litre milk
½ teaspoon ground nutmeg
1 cup (125 g/4 oz) grated
    Cheddar

1 Heat the oil in a large heavy-based pan. Add the garlic, onion, carrot, celery and mushroom. Cook, stirring, over medium heat for 2–3 minutes, or until the onion has softened. Increase the heat, add the mince and stir for a further 3–4 minutes, or until the mince has browned and is well broken up.
2 Add the tomato passata, oregano and 2 cups (500 ml/16 fl oz) water. Bring to the boil, stirring, then lower the heat and simmer for 1 hour, or until the mixture has thickened. Stir occasionally.

3 To make the cheese sauce, melt the butter in a heavy-based pan. Add the flour and cook, stirring, for 1 minute until pale and foaming. Remove from the heat, gradually add the milk and stir until smooth. Return to the heat and stir continuously for 3–4 minutes, or until the sauce boils and thickens. Cook over low heat for 1 minute. Stir in the nutmeg and Cheddar. Season.
4 To assemble, preheat the oven to moderate 180°C (350°F/Gas 4). Grease a 2.5 litre baking dish. Arrange four lasagne sheets over the base of the

baking dish. Spread one third of the meat mixture over the sheets, then pour over about ¾ cup (185 ml/6 fl oz) of the cheese sauce. Repeat with two more layers of each. Top with the four remaining lasagne sheets, then with the remaining sauce and finish with the Parmesan. Bake for 45 minutes, or until golden. Leave to stand for 5 minutes before serving.

NUTRITION PER SERVE
Protein 35 g; Fat 30 g; Carbohydrate 45 g; Dietary Fibre 5 g; Cholesterol 110 mg; 2560 kJ (610 cal)

When the mince has browned, add the passata, water and oregano.

Cook, stirring, until the sauce thickens, then add the nutmeg and Cheddar.

Finish layering with the last four sheets of lasagne, the sauce and the Parmesan.

PORK AND VEAL PIE

Preparation time: 40 minutes +
  30 minutes refrigeration
Total cooking time: 1 hour
  40 minutes
Serves 8

2 sheets ready-rolled shortcrust
  pastry
2 tablespoons oil
1 onion, finely chopped
1 clove garlic, crushed
1 kg (2 lb) lean pork and veal
  mince
2 tablespoons chopped fresh
  parsley leaves
2 tablespoons chopped fresh
  thyme leaves
2 eggs
4 cups (320 g/11 oz) fresh white
  breadcrumbs
4 gherkins, roughly chopped
125 g (4 oz) ham steak, diced
1 sheet ready-rolled puff pastry

1 Grease a shallow 22½ cm (9 inch) flan tin. Cut one sheet of pastry in half and join to the other pastry sheet, pressing the join together. Line the base and side of the tin and trim the edge. Refrigerate for 30 minutes. Preheat the oven to moderately hot 200°C (400°F/Gas 6).
2 Put the flan tin on a baking tray. Cover the base of the pastry with baking paper and baking beads or rice. Bake blind for 10 minutes, then remove the paper and beads and bake for a further 10–15 minutes, or until lightly browned. Allow to cool.
3 Heat the oil in a frying pan and fry the onion and garlic over medium heat for 5 minutes, or until soft. Remove from the heat. Combine the mince, herbs, ¼ cup (60 ml/2 fl oz) water, 1 egg and the breadcrumbs in a food processor until fine but not smooth. Place in a bowl and add the onion mixture, gherkins and ham. Season well. Mix well and fry a small amount of mixture to taste for seasoning.
4 Press the mixture firmly into the cold pastry base, forming a dome shape. Lightly beat the remaining egg and brush the edges of the pastry. Place the puff pastry over the mince to make a lid, and press the edges firmly to seal. Trim any excess pastry.

5 Brush the pastry all over with the rest of the egg and make two small slashes in the top of the pie. Using the back of a knife, decorate the top of the pie with a lattice pattern.
6 Bake for 20 minutes, then reduce the oven to moderate 180°C (350°F/Gas 4) and bake for 50 minutes, or until the pastry is golden brown. Serve cold with salad and pickles.

NUTRITION PER SERVE
Protein 40 g; Fat 25 g; Carbohydrate 55 g; Dietary Fibre 3.5 g; Cholesterol 170 mg; 2625 kJ (625 cal)

Cut one piece of shortcrust pastry in half and join to the other sheet of pastry.

Press the meat mixture into the pastry base, forming a dome shape.

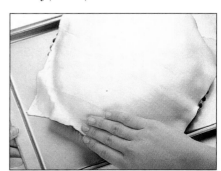

Cover with the puff pastry and press the edges of the two pastries firmly together.

MINI FRITTATAS

Preparation time: 30 minutes
Total cooking time: 45 minutes
Makes 12

1 kg (2 lb) orange sweet potato
1 tablespoon oil
30 g (1 oz) butter
4 leeks, white part only, finely
    sliced
2 cloves garlic, crushed
250 g (8 oz) feta, crumbled
8 eggs
1/2 cup (125 ml/4 fl oz) cream

1 Preheat the oven to moderate 180°C (350°F/Gas 4). Grease or brush a tray of twelve 1-cup (125 ml/4 fl oz) muffin holes with oil or melted butter. Cut small rounds of baking paper and place into the base of each hole. Cut the sweet potato into small cubes and boil, steam or microwave until tender. Drain well and set aside.

2 Heat the oil and butter in a frying pan and cook the leek for 10 minutes, stirring occasionally, or until very soft and lightly golden. Add the garlic and cook for a further 1 minute. Cool, then stir in the feta and sweet potato. Divide the mixture among the muffin holes.

3 Whisk the eggs and cream together and season with salt and cracked black pepper. Pour the egg mixture into each hole until three-quarters filled, then press the vegetables down gently. Bake for 25–30 minutes, or until golden and set. Leave in the tins for 5 minutes, then ease out with a knife. Delicious served warm or at room temperature.

NUTRITION PER FRITTATA
Protein 10 g; Fat 15 g; Carbohydrate 13 g; Dietary Fibre 2.5 g; Cholesterol 155 mg; 1000 kJ (240 cal)

Cut small rounds of baking paper and put one in the base of each muffin hole.

Spoon the vegetable mixture evenly into the muffin holes.

Whisk the eggs and cream together, season and pour into the muffin holes.

Use the back of a large metal spoon to lightly crush the peppercorns.

Beat the egg whites and caster sugar until the mixture turns white and thickens.

Fold the flour, spices, almonds and peppercorns into the egg white mixture.

Cut the bread into thin slices and arrange them in a single layer on baking trays.

PEPPER AND ALMOND BREAD

Preparation time: 10 minutes +
 3 hours standing
Total cooking time: 1 hour 10 minutes
Makes about 70 pieces

2 teaspoons black peppercorns
2 egg whites
1/3 cup (90 g/3 oz) caster sugar
3/4 cup (90 g/3 oz) plain flour
1/4 teaspoon ground ginger
1/4 teaspoon ground cinnamon
1 cup (155 g/5 oz) almonds

1 Preheat the oven to moderate 180°C (350°F/Gas 4). Grease an 8 x 26 cm (3 x 10½ inch) bar tin. Line the base and sides with baking paper. Lightly crush the peppercorns with the back of a metal spoon or in a mortar and pestle.

2 Beat the egg whites and sugar with electric beaters for 4 minutes, or until the mixture turns white and thickens. Sift the flour, ginger and cinnamon and fold in with the almonds and crushed peppercorns.

3 Spread the mixture into the tin. Bake for 35 minutes, or until lightly browned. Cool in the tin for at least 3 hours, before turning out onto a board. (You can wrap the bread in foil and slice the next day at this stage.) Using a serrated knife, cut the bread into 3 mm (1/8 inch) slices. Place the slices in a single layer on baking trays. Bake in a slow 150°C (300°F/Gas 2) oven for about 25–35 minutes, or until the slices are dry and crisp. Allow to cool completely before serving.

NUTRITION PER PIECE
Protein 1 g; Fat 1.5 g; Carbohydrate 2.5 g; Dietary Fibre 0 g; Cholesterol 0 mg; 95 kJ (25 cal)

COOK'S FILE

Note: To make traditional almond bread, simply remove the peppercorns.

69

PORK PIES

Preparation time: 20 minutes
Total cooking time: 1 hour 15 minutes
Makes 6

400 g (13 oz) pork mince
1/4 cup (35 g/1 1/4 oz) shelled
    pistachios, chopped
1/2 apple, finely chopped
1 teaspoon finely chopped
    sage leaves
2 1/4 cups (280 g/9 oz)
    plain flour
80 g (2 3/4 oz) butter
1 egg, lightly beaten
1 egg yolk
1/2 cup (125 ml/4 fl oz)
    vegetable stock
1/2 cup (125 ml/4 fl oz)
    unsweetened apple juice
1 1/2 teaspoons gelatine

1 Preheat the oven to moderately hot 200°C (400°F/Gas 6). Combine the mince, pistachios, apple and sage in a large bowl and season very well with salt and cracked black pepper. Fry a teaspoon of the filling and adjust the seasoning if necessary. Cover and refrigerate until needed.

2 Put the flour and 1/2 teaspoon of salt in a large bowl and make a well in the centre. Put the butter in a small pan with 1/3 cup (100 ml/3 fl oz) of water and bring to the boil. Pour into the centre of the well, add the beaten egg and mix to form a smooth dough.

3 Grease six 1/3-cup (80 ml/2 3/4 fl oz) capacity muffin holes. Set aside one third of the dough and divide the rest into six portions. Roll each portion into a small circle and line the muffin cups with the dough, leaving a little dough hanging over the side of each

cup. Divide the filling among the pastry-filled cups, packing the filling down and making a small dome shape in the centre—the filling will shrink as it cooks. Divide the remaining dough into six portions and roll each into a small circle to make the lids. Brush the edges with water and lay one on top of each pie. Fold up the pastry hanging over the edge and roll or crimp it. Cut a small hole in the top of each pie. Brush with the egg yolk mixed with a tablespoon of water.

4 Put the muffin tin on a baking tray and bake for 30 minutes; then check the pastry top. If they are still pale, bake for another 5–10 minutes. Leave to rest for 5 minutes, then lift the pies out of the muffin tray, put them on the baking tray and bake for 15 minutes, or until the sides of the pies are golden brown (be careful not to break the pies when you move them).

5 Bring the stock and half the apple juice to the boil in a small pan. Sprinkle the gelatine over the surface of the remaining apple juice and leave to go spongy, then pour on the boiling stock and mix until the gelatine dissolves. Place a small funnel (a piping nozzle works well) in the hole of each pie and pour in a little of the gelatine mixture. Leave to settle, then pour in a little more until the pies are full. It is important to fill the pies completely to make sure there are no gaps when the gelatine mixture sets. You may need more or less liquid, depending on how much the meat shrinks. Allow to cool completely before serving.

NUTRITION PER PIE
Protein 25 g; Fat 17 g; Carbohydrate 32 g; Dietary Fibre 2.5 g; Cholesterol 25 mg; 1565 kJ (375 cal)

Mix together the mince, pistachios, apple and sage and season with salt and pepper.

Bring the melted butter and water to the boil and pour into the centre of the well.

Line the muffin holes, leaving a little dough hanging over the sides.

Spoon the filling into the pastry shells and pack firmly into a dome shape.

Put the dough lids on top, then fold up the pastry hanging over the side and roll it.

Put a funnel in the hole of the pie and pour in some of the gelatine mixture.

CAPONATA

Preparation time: 20 minutes +
  24 hours refrigeration
Total cooking time: 40 minutes
Serves 8

1 kg (2 lb) eggplant, cubed
3/4 cup (185 ml/6 fl oz) olive oil
200 g (6½ oz) zucchini, cubed
1 red capsicum, thinly sliced
2 onions, finely sliced
4 celery sticks, sliced
400 g (13 oz) can crushed
    tomatoes
3 tablespoons red wine vinegar
2 tablespoons sugar
2 tablespoons drained capers
24 green olives, pitted
2 tablespoons pine nuts, toasted

1 Put the eggplant in a colander, add 2 teaspoons of salt and leave to drain.
2 Heat 3 tablespoons of the oil in a large frying pan and fry the zucchini and capsicum for 5–6 minutes, or until the zucchini is lightly browned. Transfer to a bowl. Add a little more oil to the pan and gently fry the onion and celery for 6–8 minutes, or until softened but not brown. Transfer to the bowl.
3 Rinse the eggplant and pat dry. Add ¼ cup (60 ml/2 fl oz) of the oil to the pan, increase the heat and brown the eggplant in batches. Keep adding more oil to each batch. Drain on paper towels and set aside.
4 Remove any excess oil from the pan and return the vegetables to the pan, except the eggplant.
5 Add ¼ cup (60 ml/2 fl oz) water and the tomatoes. Reduce the heat and simmer for 10 minutes. Add the remaining ingredients and eggplant and mix well. Remove from the heat and cool. Cover and leave for 24 hours in the refrigerator. Add some pepper, and more vinegar if needed.

NUTRITION PER SERVE
Protein 3.5 g; Fat 25 g; Carbohydrate 8.5 g; Dietary Fibre 5.5 g; Cholesterol 0 mg; 1160 kJ (280 cal)

COOK'S FILE

Note: Green olives stuffed with red pimentos can be used instead of pitted green olives.
Storage time: Caponata will keep, covered, in the refrigerator for up to 5 days.

You can remove the stones from the olives with an olive pitter.

Increase the heat and brown the eggplant in the oil in batches.

Add the water and crushed tomatoes to the pan and simmer.

OCTOPUS IN RED WINE

Preparation time: 25 minutes
Total cooking time: 35 minutes
Serves 8

2 kg (4 lb) baby octopus
1 cup (250 ml/8 fl oz) dry
    red wine
1/4 cup (55 g/2 oz) soft brown
    sugar
2 bay leaves
2 sprigs fresh oregano
1/2 cup (125 ml/4 fl oz) olive oil

1/3 cup (80 ml/2³/4 fl oz) red
    wine vinegar
1/2 cup (15 g/1/2 oz) chopped
    fresh flat-leaf parsley
1 clove garlic, crushed

1 Remove the octopus head from the tentacles with a sharp knife, cut off the eyes and carefully slit the head open. Remove the gut and cut the head in half. Push out the beak from the centre of the tentacles. Cut the tentacles into sets of two or four, depending on the size. Pull away the skin from the head and tentacles if it comes away easily.

2 Place the octopus, red wine, sugar, bay leaves and oregano in a large pan. Cover and simmer for 35 minutes, or until the octopus is tender.

3 Drain the octopus, discard the herbs and place in a bowl. Leave to cool for 10 minutes.

4 Add the oil, vinegar, parsley and garlic to the octopus and mix well. Serve at room temperature as part of an antipasto platter or with a salad.

NUTRITION PER SERVE
Protein 40 g; Fat 18 g; Carbohydrate 6.5 g; Dietary Fibre 0 g; Cholesterol 498 mg; 1574 kJ (375 cal)

To clean the octopus, remove the head from the tentacles and cut off the eyes.

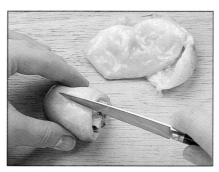

Carefully slit open the head and remove the gut.

Use your fingers to push out the beak from the centre of the tentacles.

HOKKIEN NOODLE SALAD

Preparation time: 20 minutes
Total cooking time: Nil
Serves 8

900 g (1³/4 lb) Hokkien noodles
6 spring onions, sliced
   diagonally
1 large red capsicum, thinly
   sliced
200 g (6¹/2 oz) snow peas,
   finely sliced
1 carrot, sliced diagonally
50 g (1²/3 oz) fresh mint,
   chopped
50 g (1²/3 oz) fresh coriander,
   chopped
100 g (3¹/2 oz) roasted cashew
   nuts

Sesame Dressing
2 teaspoons sesame oil
1 tablespoon peanut oil
2 tablespoons lime juice
2 tablespoons kecap manis
   (see Note)
3 tablespoons sweet chilli sauce

1 Gently separate the noodles and place in a large bowl, cover with boiling water and leave for 2 minutes. Rinse and drain.
2 Put the noodles in a large bowl, and add spring onions, capsicum, snow peas, carrot, mint and coriander. Toss to combine.
3 To make the dressing, whisk together the oils, lime juice, kecap manis and sweet chilli sauce. Pour the dressing over the salad and toss again. Sprinkle the cashew nuts over the top and serve immediately.

NUTRITION PER SERVE
Protein 10 g; Fat 9 g; Carbohydrate 35 g; Dietary Fibre 4.5 g; Cholesterol 0 mg; 1115 kJ (265 cal)

COOK'S FILE

Note: If kecap manis is unavailable, use soy sauce sweetened with a little soft brown sugar.

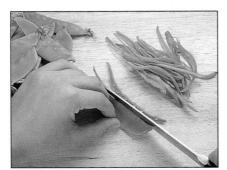

Top and tail the snow peas, then finely slice lengthways with a sharp knife.

Separate the noodles, then put them in a large bowl and cover with boiling water.

Whisk together the oils, lime juice, kecap manis and sweet chilli sauce.

COUSCOUS PATTIES

Preparation time: 35 minutes +
 15 minutes refrigeration +
 10 minutes standing
Total cooking time: 30 minutes
Makes 4

1 cup (185 g/6 oz) couscous
4 tablespoons oil
1 eggplant, finely diced
1 onion, finely chopped
1 clove garlic, crushed
2 teaspoons ground cumin
2 teaspoons ground coriander
1 red capsicum, finely diced
2 tablespoons chopped fresh
 coriander

2 teaspoons grated lemon rind
2 teaspoons lemon juice
5 tablespoons natural yoghurt
1 egg, lightly beaten
oil, for shallow-frying

1 Place the couscous in a bowl. Add 1 cup (250 ml/8 fl oz) of boiling water and leave for 10 minutes, or until all the water has been absorbed. Fluff up the grains with a fork.
2 Heat 2 tablespoons of the oil in a large frying pan and fry the eggplant until soft and golden, then place in a bowl. Heat 1 tablespoon of the oil in the pan. Add the onion, garlic, cumin and ground coriander. Cook over medium heat for 3–4 minutes, or until soft, then add to the bowl.

Heat the remaining oil and cook the capsicum for 5 minutes, or until soft. Place in the bowl and stir well.
3 Add the vegetable mixture to the couscous with the fresh coriander, lemon rind, lemon juice, yoghurt and egg. Season to taste and mix well.
4 Using damp hands, divide the mixture into four portions and form into large patties—they should be about 2 cm (3/4 inch) thick. Cover and refrigerate for 15 minutes. Shallow-fry the patties over medium heat for 5 minutes on each side, or until golden. Drain well and serve with yoghurt.

NUTRITION PER PATTY
Protein 9 g; Fat 25 g; Carbohydrate 35 g; Dietary Fibre 4 g; Cholesterol 5 mg; 1760 kJ (420 cal)

When the couscous has absorbed the water, fluff up the grains with a fork.

Season the patty mixture with salt and cracked pepper and mix well.

With damp hands, form the mixture into four large patties.

Pasta Sauces

These delicious recipes should be served with 500 g (1 lb) of cooked pasta which will give you four good-sized portions. Long thin pastas are traditionally served with thin oily sauces, while the shorter fatter pastas hold chunky sauces better, but feel free to experiment to suit your own tastes.

TOMATO SAUCE

Heat 1 tablespoon olive oil in a large frying pan. Add 1 finely chopped onion and 1 crushed clove garlic and cook over medium heat for 5 minutes, or until softened. Stir in 2 x 400 g (13 oz) cans chopped tomatoes and 2 tablespoons tomato paste and simmer for 10 minutes, or until the sauce has reduced and thickened. Season with plenty of salt and cracked pepper. Stir in 1/4 cup (7 g/1/4 oz) fresh shredded basil leaves and cook for 1 minute. Pour over cooked pasta and top with grated Parmesan.

NUTRITION PER SERVE (4)
Protein 8.5 g; Fat 7 g; Carbohydrate 35 g; Dietary Fibre 4.5 g; Cholesterol 5 mg; 1020 kJ (245 cal)

CREAMY PUMPKIN AND PINE NUT SAUCE

Chop 1.5 kg (3 lb) butternut pumpkin into 3–5 cm (1–2 inch) cubes. Place in a pan with 1 litre chicken or vegetable stock and cook, covered, for approximately 10–15 minutes, or until the pumpkin is soft enough to mash. Heat 3 tablespoons oil and fry 2 chopped onions, 2 finely chopped cloves garlic and 1 large celery stalk, sliced, until the onions are cooked and lightly browned. Add 2 teaspoons ground cumin, 1/2 teaspoon ground cinnamon, 1 teaspoon paprika, 1/4 teaspoon nutmeg and cook for a further 2 minutes, or until aromatic. Cool the pumpkin slightly and place in a food processor or blender.

Add the onion mixture and process until smooth. Add 1/2 cup (125 ml/ 4 fl oz) cream and season to taste. Serve over pasta and sprinkle with 1/4 cup (15 g/1/2 oz) chopped fresh parsley and 1/3 cup (50 g/1 3/4 oz) toasted pine nuts.

NUTRITION PER SERVE (4)
Protein 15 g; Fat 40 g; Carbohydrate 60 g; Dietary Fibre 9 g; Cholesterol 45 mg; 2795 kJ (660 cal)

PUTTANESCA SAUCE

Heat 2 tablespoons olive oil in a large heavy-based pan. Add 3 crushed cloves garlic, 2 tablespoons chopped fresh parsley, 1/2 teaspoon chilli flakes and 1 tablespoon chopped fresh oregano. Cook, stirring constantly, for

1 minute over medium heat. Add two 425 g (14 oz) cans chopped tomatoes and bring to the boil, then simmer, covered, for 5 minutes. Add 1 tablespoon rinsed and drained capers, 3 thinly sliced anchovy fillets and ¼ cup (45 g/1½ oz) black olives and cook, stirring, for 5 minutes. Season with salt and cracked black pepper and serve with spaghetti.

NUTRITION PER SERVE (4)
Protein 8 g; Fat 10 g; Carbohydrate 40 g; Dietary Fibre 6 g; Cholesterol 2 mg; 1195 kJ (285 cal)

CREAMED MUSHROOM AND CHIVE SAUCE

Heat 50 g (1¾ oz) butter in a large deep frying pan until it sizzles. Add 1 finely chopped onion and cook until soft and golden. Add 3 crushed cloves garlic and cook for 1 minute. Remove the skins of 400 g (13 oz) field mushrooms and roughly chop. Add the mushrooms to the pan and cook, stirring, for about 5 minutes, or until tender. Add 1 cup (250 ml/8 fl oz) cream and bring to the boil. Reduce the heat and simmer for 4 minutes, or until slightly

From left to right: Tomato sauce; Creamy pumpkin and pine nut sauce; Puttanesca sauce; Blue cheese sauce; Bolognese sauce; Creamed mushroom and chive sauce.

reduced and thickened. Remove from the heat and stir through ½ cup (60 g/2¼ oz) grated vintage Cheddar. Stir through ⅓ cup (20 g/¾ oz) chives cut into 2 cm (¾ inch) lengths. Season to taste before serving.

NUTRITION PER SERVE (4)
Protein 15 g; Fat 45 g; Carbohydrate 35 g; Dietary Fibre 5.5 g; Cholesterol 130 mg; 2435 kJ (580 cal)

BOLOGNESE SAUCE

Heat 2 tablespoons olive oil in a large deep pan. Add 2 crushed cloves garlic, 1 chopped onion, carrot and celery stick. Cook, stirring, for 5 minutes over low heat until the vegetables are golden. Increase the heat and add 500 g (1 lb) beef mince and brown well, stirring and breaking up any lumps as it cooks. Add 2 cups (500 ml/16 fl oz) beef stock, 1½ cups (375 ml/12 fl oz) red wine, 2 x 425 g (14 oz) cans crushed tomatoes, 1 teaspoon sugar and ¼ cup (15 g/½ oz) finely chopped fresh parsley. Bring to the boil, reduce the heat and simmer,

uncovered, for about 1½ hours, stirring occasionally. Season well and serve with spaghetti.

NUTRITION PER SERVE (4)
Protein 40 g; Fat 30 g; Carbohydrate 50 g; Dietary Fibre 7 g; Cholesterol 110 mg; 2740kJ (655 cal)

BLUE CHEESE SAUCE

Heat 1 tablespoon olive oil in a shallow frying pan. Add 1 small finely chopped onion and 2 crushed cloves garlic and cook, stirring, until the onion is soft. Add 1 cup (250 ml/8 fl oz) cream and bring to the boil. Add 300 g (10 oz) crumbled blue cheese and simmer over low heat until the cheese has melted. Simmer for a further 3 minutes, or until the sauce has thickened slightly. Season to taste. Pour the sauce over hot gnocchi and gently toss through. Sprinkle with grated Parmesan and cracked pepper.

NUTRITION PER SERVE (4)
Protein 20 g; Fat 55 g; Carbohydrate 35 g; Dietary Fibre 3 g; Cholesterol 160 mg; 3030 kJ (725 cal)

PUMPKIN AND PESTO CHICKEN IN FILO PASTRY

Preparation time: 30 minutes
Total cooking time: 50 minutes
Serves 4

4 chicken breast fillets
1 tablespoon oil
250 g (8 oz) pumpkin
1 bunch English spinach
12 sheets filo pastry
100 g (3½ oz) butter, melted
¼ cup (25 g/¾ oz) dry
  breadcrumbs
100 g (3½ oz) ricotta
⅓ cup (90 g/3 oz) pesto
  (see Note)
1 tablespoon pine nuts, chopped

1 Preheat the oven to moderately hot 200°C (400°F/Gas 6). Season the chicken fillets with salt and pepper. Heat half the oil in a frying pan and fry the chicken until browned on both sides, then remove from the pan.
2 Cut the peeled pumpkin into 5 mm (¼ inch) slices. Heat the remaining oil in the same pan and fry the pumpkin until lightly browned on both sides. Allow to cool.
3 Put the spinach leaves into a pan of boiling water and stir until just wilted. Drain well and pat dry with paper towels. Layer 3 sheets of filo pastry, brushing each with some of the melted butter, sprinkling between layers with some of the breadcrumbs.
4 Wrap each chicken breast in a quarter of the spinach and place on one short side of the filo, leaving a gap of about 2 cm (¾ inch). Top the chicken with a quarter of the pumpkin slices, then spread a quarter of the

ricotta down the centre of the pumpkin. Top with a tablespoon of the pesto.
5 Fold the sides of the pastry over the filling, then roll the parcel up until it sits on the unsecured end. Repeat with the remaining ingredients. Place the parcels on a lightly greased baking tray, brush with any remaining butter and sprinkle with the pine nuts. Bake for 15 minutes, cover loosely with foil and bake for a

further 20 minutes, or until the pastry is golden brown.

NUTRITION PER SERVE
Protein 35 g; Fat 40 g; Carbohydrate 30 g; Dietary Fibre 2.5 g; Cholesterol 132 mg; 2635 kJ (630 cal)

COOK'S FILE

Note: Bottled pesto is not suitable for this recipe—you can either make your own (see page 56) or use fresh pesto from a deli.

Remove the spinach from the boiling water and drain well.

Top the chicken with a quarter of the pumpkin slices.

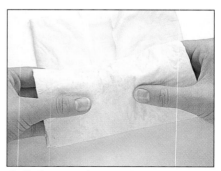

Roll the parcel up until it sits on the unsecured end.

BLUE CHEESE AND ONION FLAN

Preparation time: 40 minutes +
  20 minutes refrigeration
Total cooking time: 1 hour 40 minutes
Serves 8

2 tablespoons olive oil
1 kg (2 lb) red onions, very
  thinly sliced
1 teaspoon soft brown sugar
2 cups (250 g/8 oz) plain flour
100 g (3^1/$_2$ oz) cold butter, cubed
^{3}/$_4$ cup (180 ml/6 fl oz) cream
3 eggs
100 g (3^1/$_2$ oz) blue cheese,
  crumbled

1 teaspoon freshly chopped
  lemon thyme or thyme leaves

1 Heat the oil in a heavy-based pan over low heat. Add the onion and sugar and cook, stirring regularly, for 45 minutes, or until the onion is soft and lightly golden.
2 Process the flour and butter in a food processor for 15 seconds. Add 1–2 tablespoons of iced water and process in short bursts until the mixture just comes together. Turn out onto a floured surface and gather into a ball. Cover with plastic wrap and refrigerate for 10 minutes.
3 Preheat the oven to moderate 180°C (350°F/Gas 4). Roll out the pastry thinly on a lightly floured surface to

fit a greased 22 cm (8^3/$_4$ inch) round loose-based flan tin. Trim any excess pastry. Chill for 10 minutes. Line with crumpled baking paper and fill with baking beads or rice. Put on a baking tray and bake for 10 minutes. Remove the paper and beads, then bake for 10 minutes, or until lightly golden and dry.
4 Cool, then gently spread the onion over the base of the pastry shell. Whisk together the cream, eggs, blue cheese, thyme and pepper to taste. Pour into the pastry shell and bake for 35 minutes, or until firm.

NUTRITION PER SERVE
Protein 9 g; Fat 30 g; Carbohydrate 25 g; Dietary Fibre 1.5 g; Cholesterol 145 mg; 1718 kJ (410 cal)

Turn the dough out onto a lightly floured surface and gather into a ball.

Roll the pastry out thinly and line the greased flan tin, trimming away any excess.

Spread the onion over the cooled pastry base, then pour in the cream mixture.

CHICKEN BALLOTINE

Preparation time: 40 minutes
Total cooking time: 1 hour 45 minutes
Serves 8

1.6 kg (3¼ lb) whole chicken
2 red capsicums
1 bunch silverbeet
30 g (1 oz) butter
1 onion, finely chopped
1 clove garlic, crushed
½ cup (50 g/1¾ oz) grated
    Parmesan
1 cup (80 g/2¾ oz) fresh
    breadcrumbs
1 tablespoon chopped fresh
    oregano
200 g (6½ oz) ricotta

1 To bone the chicken, cut through the skin on the centre back with a sharp knife. Separate the flesh from the bone down one side to the breast, being careful not to pierce the skin. Follow along the bones closely with the knife, gradually easing the meat from the thigh, drumstick and wing. Cut through the thigh bone where it meets the drumstick and cut off the wing tip. Repeat on the other side, then lift the rib cage away, leaving the flesh in one piece and the drumsticks still attached to the flesh. Scrape all the meat from the drumstick and wings, discarding the bones. Turn the wing and drumstick flesh inside the chicken and lay the chicken out flat, skin-side-down. Refrigerate.

2 Preheat the oven to moderate 180°C (350°F/Gas 4). Quarter the capsicums and remove the membranes and seeds. Place skin-side-up under a hot grill until the skin blisters and blackens. Place in a plastic bag and allow to cool, then peel off the skin.

3 Remove the stalks from the silverbeet and finely shred the leaves. Melt the butter in a large frying pan and add the onion and garlic. Cook over medium heat for about 5 minutes, or until soft. Add the silverbeet leaves and stir until wilted and all the moisture has evaporated. In a food processor, process the silverbeet and onion mixture with the Parmesan, breadcrumbs, oregano and half the ricotta. Season to taste with salt and cracked pepper.

4 Spread the spinach mixture over the chicken and lay the capsicum over the spinach. Form the remaining ricotta into a roll and place across the width of the chicken. Fold the sides of the chicken in over the filling so they overlap slightly and tuck the ends in neatly. Secure with toothpicks and tie with string at 3 cm (1¼ inch) intervals.

5 Lightly grease a large piece of foil and place the chicken in the centre. Roll the chicken up securely in the foil, sealing the ends well. Place on a baking tray and bake for 1¼–1½ hours, or until the juices run clear when a skewer is inserted into the centre. Allow to cool, then refrigerate until cold before removing the foil, toothpicks and string. Cut into 1 cm (½ inch) slices to serve.

NUTRITION PER SERVE
Protein 40 g; Fat 12 g; Carbohydrate 9 g; Dietary Fibre 1.5 g; Cholesterol 105 mg; 1290 kJ (310 cal)

COOK'S FILE

Note: If you are not confident about boning a chicken, ask your butcher to do it for you. To be on the safe side, it might be worth ordering your boned chicken a day in advance.

Using a sharp knife, cut through the skin on the centre back.

Separate the flesh from the bone down one side to the breast.

With your knife, gradually ease the meat from the thigh, drumstick and wing.

Use a sharp knife to cut off the wing tips through the joint.

Lay the chicken out flat and cover with the spinach mixture and capsicum quarters.

Roll the chicken up to enclose the filling and secure with toothpicks.

ORANGE ROASTED CHICKENS

Preparation time: 15 minutes +
  3 hours refrigeration
Total cooking time: 40 minutes
Serves 8

2 x 800 g (1 lb 10 oz) chickens
100 g (3½ oz) butter,
  softened
2 cloves garlic, crushed
1 tablespoon finely grated
  orange rind
3 tablespoons orange juice

1 Preheat the oven to hot 220°C (425°F/Gas 7). Using kitchen scissors, cut the chickens in half through the back and breast bone. Pat dry with paper towels and wipe out the inside.
2 Combine the butter, garlic and orange rind and beat well. Gently loosen the skin of the chickens by sliding your fingers between the flesh and the skin. Push the orange butter under the skin as evenly as possible. Put the chickens onto a ceramic dish and pour on the orange juice. Cover with plastic wrap and refrigerate for 3 hours, or preferably overnight. Drain well.

3 Arrange the chicken pieces cut-side-down on roasting racks inside two baking dishes. Pour 2 tablespoons of water into each baking dish.
4 Roast for 30–40 minutes, or until the chickens are golden brown. Cover with foil and allow to rest for 15 minutes. Cut into quarters to serve.

NUTRITION PER SERVE
Protein 30 g; Fat 15 g; Carbohydrate 1 g; Dietary Fibre 0 g; Cholesterol 95 mg; 990 kJ (235 cal)

COOK'S FILE

Hint: If you can, use freshly squeezed orange juice.

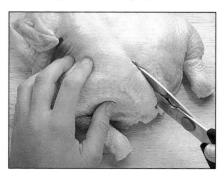

Cut the chickens in half through the back bone and breast bone.

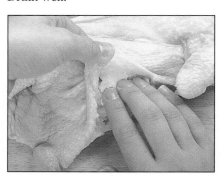

Loosen the skin of both chickens and spread the orange butter underneath.

Put the chicken pieces cut-side-down on the roasting racks inside baking dishes.

BAKED HERBED FETA

Preparation time: 10 minutes
Total cooking time: 15 minutes
Serves 6

300 g (10 oz) piece of feta
1 tablespoon chopped fresh
    rosemary
1 tablespoon chopped fresh
    oregano
1 tablespoon chopped fresh thyme
2 tablespoons olive oil

1 Preheat the oven to moderate 180°C (350°F/Gas 4). Put the feta on a piece of foil about 30 cm (12 inches) square. Mix together the rosemary, oregano and thyme, and press onto the sides of the feta. Drizzle with the oil and season to taste with cracked black pepper. Gently fold the sides and ends of the foil over to make a parcel.
2 Place on a baking tray and bake for 10–15 minutes, or until the feta is soft. Drain any excess liquid before serving. Serve either hot or cold, chopped in salads, with bread or as part of a cheese platter.

NUTRITION PER SERVE
Protein 9 g; Fat 20 g; Carbohydrate 0 g; Dietary Fibre 0 g; Cholesterol 35 mg; 820 kJ (195 cal)

COOK'S FILE

Note: If the piece of feta is thick, it may need an extra 5 minutes in the oven to heat through.
Storage: Cover any leftovers with plastic wrap and store in the fridge for up to 2 days.

Using a sharp knife, finely chop the rosemary, oregano and thyme.

Press the combined herbs onto the sides of the feta.

Fold the foil firmly over the feta to make a secure parcel.

THAI CHICKEN BALLS

Preparation time: 20 minutes
Total cooking time: 40 minutes
Serves 6

1 kg (2 lb) chicken mince
1 cup (80 g/2³/4 oz) fresh
    breadcrumbs
4 spring onions, sliced
1 tablespoon ground coriander
1 cup (50 g/1³/4 oz) chopped
    fresh coriander

3 tablespoons sweet chilli sauce
1–2 tablespoons lemon juice
oil, for frying

1 Preheat the oven to moderately hot 200°C (400°F/Gas 6). Mix the mince and breadcrumbs in a large bowl.
2 Add the spring onion, ground and fresh coriander, chilli sauce and lemon juice and mix well. Using damp hands, form the mixture into evenly shaped balls that are either small enough to eat with your fingers or large enough to use as burgers.

3 Heat the oil in a deep frying pan, and shallow-fry the chicken balls in batches over high heat until browned all over. Place them on a baking tray and bake until cooked through. (The small chicken balls will take 5 minutes to cook and the larger ones will take 10–15 minutes.) This mixture also makes a delicious filling for sausage rolls.

NUTRITION PER SERVE
Protein 40 g; Fat 8 g; Carbohydrate 10 g; Dietary Fibre 1 g; Cholesterol 85 mg; 1160 kJ (275 cal)

Mix the spring onion, coriander, chilli sauce and lemon juice into the mince mixture.

With damp hands, form the mixture into evenly shaped balls.

Fry the chicken balls in oil until they are browned on both sides.

PIZZA-TOPPED FOCACCIA

Preparation time: 30 minutes +
 1 hour 30 minutes standing
Total cooking time: 40 minutes
Serves 4

7 g (¼ oz) dried yeast
1 teaspoon sugar
2 tablespoons olive oil
2½ cups (310 g/10 oz) plain
    flour, sifted

Pizza Topping
1 tablespoon tomato paste
1 large red capsicum,
    thinly sliced
125 g (4 oz) marinated
    artichoke hearts, quartered
¼ cup (30 g/1 oz) black olives,
    pitted
200 g (6½ oz) bocconcini,
    thickly sliced

1 Combine the yeast, ¾ cup (185 ml/ 6 fl oz) of warm water and the sugar in a bowl and set aside in a warm place for 5–10 minutes, or until frothy. Put the oil, flour and 1 teaspoon salt in a large bowl, add the frothy yeast and mix to a soft dough.
2 Turn the dough out onto a lightly floured surface and knead for 10 minutes, or until smooth and elastic. Form into a ball and place in a large oiled bowl. Cover with oiled plastic wrap and set aside in a warm place for 1 hour, or until doubled in size.
3 Preheat the oven to moderate 180°C (350°F/Gas 4). Punch down the dough with your fist to expel any air, and knead for 1 minute. Roll into a flat disc large enough to fit into a greased 23 cm (9 inch) springform tin. Press

into the tin, cover with a tea towel and leave to rise for about 20 minutes.
4 Spread the tomato paste over the dough, and arrange the other topping ingredients, except for the bocconcini, on top. Bake for 20 minutes, remove from the oven and spread the slices of bocconcini over the top, then bake for

a further 20 minutes, or until the dough is well risen and firm to the touch in the centre. Cool on a wire rack before cutting and serving.

NUTRITION PER SERVE
Protein 25 g; Fat 20 g; Carbohydrate 60 g; Dietary Fibre 5 g; Cholesterol 30 mg; 2235 kJ (535 cal)

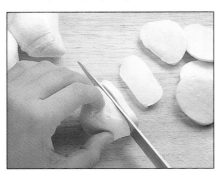

Cut the bocconcini into thick slices with a sharp knife.

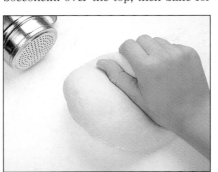

On a lightly floured surface, knead the dough until smooth and elastic.

Arrange the capsicum, artichokes and olives over the tomato paste.

MARINATED BOCCONCINI

Preparation time: 15 minutes +
   3 days refrigeration
Total cooking time: 5 minutes
Serves 8

400 g (13 oz) bocconcini, sliced
150 g (5 oz) jar sun-dried
   capsicums in oil
1 cup (50 g/1¾ oz) small fresh
   basil leaves
1¼ cups (315 ml/10 fl oz) extra
   virgin olive oil
¼ cup (60 ml/2 fl oz) lemon juice

1 Dry the bocconcini with paper towels. Drain the capsicums, retaining the oil in a pan, and cut into strips. Gently crush the basil leaves. Pour 1 cup (250 ml/8 fl oz) of the olive oil into the pan with the reserved oil and gently heat for 5 minutes. Stir the lemon juice into the warmed oil.
2 Put a layer of bocconcini slices in a wide-necked 3-cup (750 ml/24 fl oz) sterilised clip-top jar. Sprinkle with cracked pepper. Put a thin layer of basil leaves on top of the cheese and cover with some of the capsicum. Continue layering, then cover with the warmed oil, using the remaining olive oil if necessary. Seal the jar and marinate in the refrigerator for 3 days. Return to room temperature and drain before serving.

NUTRITION PER SERVE
Protein 13 g; Fat 25 g; Carbohydrate 1 g;
Dietary Fibre 0 g; Cholesterol 30 mg;
1194 kJ (285 cal)

COOK'S FILE

Note: To sterilise a storage jar, rinse with boiling water then place in a warm oven until completely dry.

Drain the oil from the capsicums into a small pan.

Gently crush the basil leaves with a knife to release more of the flavour.

Continue layering the bocconcini, basil and capsicum and cover with the warmed oil.

SPICED PEARS

Preparation time: 10 minutes
Total cooking time: 1 hour
Serves 8

¹/₃ cup (80 ml/2³/₄ fl oz) kecap
   manis
3 tablespoons soy sauce
2 teaspoons sesame oil
1 teaspoon five-spice powder
6 ripe buerre bosc pears,
   unpeeled and quartered

1 Preheat the oven to slow 150°C (300°F/Gas 2). Line two shallow baking trays with foil and place a wire rack in each tray. In a large bowl, mix the kecap manis, soy sauce, sesame oil and five-spice powder.
2 Brush the quartered pears all over with the soy mixture. Place apart, skin-side-down, in a single layer on the racks. Bake for 30 minutes. Brush the pears again with the marinade and continue baking for a further 30 minutes, or until the pears are tender and caramelised around the edge.

3 Serve the pears warm or at room temperature with cheese and biscuits or as an accompaniment to cold meat.

NUTRITION PER SERVE
Protein 1 g; Fat 1 g; Carbohydrate 15 g; Dietary Fibre 2.5 g; Cholesterol 0 mg; 280 kJ (65 cal)

COOK'S FILE

Hint: The foil will catch any excess drops of the soy mixture. If the mixture scorches or burns during the cooking process, replace the foil lining halfway through the cooking time.

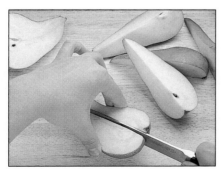

Wash but don't peel the pears, then cut them into quarters.

Mix together the kecap manis, soy sauce, sesame oil and five-spice powder.

Arrange the pears, skin-side-down, in a single layer on the wire racks.

ORANGE POPPY SEED CAKE

Preparation time: 40 minutes
+ 15 minutes standing
Total cooking time: 1 hour
Serves 12

1½ cups (185 g/6 oz) self-raising flour
⅓ cup (60 g/2 oz) ground almonds
¼ cup (40 g/1¼ oz) poppy seeds
185 g (6 oz) butter
⅔ cup (160 g/5½ oz) caster sugar
¼ cup (80 g/2¾ oz) apricot jam or marmalade
2–3 teaspoons finely grated orange rind
⅓ cup (80 ml/2¾ fl oz) orange juice
3 eggs, lightly beaten
100 g (3½ oz) butter
100 g (3½ oz) cream cheese
1 cup (125 g/4 oz) icing sugar, sifted
1 teaspoon lemon juice or vanilla essence
orange zest, to decorate

1 Preheat the oven to moderate 180°C (350°F/Gas 4). Brush a deep 20 cm (8 inch) round cake tin with melted butter or oil. Line the base and side with baking paper. Sift the flour into a bowl and add the almonds and poppy seeds. Make a well in the centre.

2 Place the butter, sugar, jam, orange rind and juice in a pan. Stir over low heat until the butter has melted and the mixture is smooth. Gradually add the butter mixture to the dry ingredients, stirring with a whisk until smooth. Add the eggs and whisk until combined.

3 Pour the mixture into the tin and bake for 50–60 minutes, or until a skewer comes out clean when inserted in the centre. Leave the cake in the tin for at least 15 minutes before turning onto a wire rack to cool.

4 To make the cream cheese icing, beat the butter and cream cheese until smooth. Add the icing sugar and lemon juice or vanilla gradually and beat until thick and creamy. Spread the icing over the cooled cake. Decorate with strips of orange zest.

NUTRITION PER SERVE
Protein 5 g; Fat 25 g; Carbohydrate 40 g; Dietary Fibre 1 g; Cholesterol 115 mg; 1715 kJ (410 cal)

Stir the butter, sugar, jam, orange rind and juice over low heat until the butter melts.

Add the beaten egg to the mixture and whisk until smooth.

Turn the cake out onto a wire rack to cool and remove the baking paper.

Blend the icing sugar and lemon juice or vanilla into the cream cheese mixture.

CHOCOLATE HAZELNUT FRIANDS

Preparation time: 20 minutes
Total cooking time: 40 minutes
Makes 12

200 g (6½ oz) whole hazelnuts
185 g (6 oz) butter
6 egg whites
1¼ cups (155 g/5 oz) plain flour
¼ cup (30 g/1 oz) cocoa powder
2 cups (250 g/8 oz) icing sugar
icing sugar, extra, to dust

1 Preheat the oven to moderately hot 200°C (400°F/Gas 6). Grease twelve ½-cup (125 ml/4 fl oz) friand or muffin holes. Spread the hazelnuts out on a baking tray and bake for 8–10 minutes, or until fragrant (take care not to burn). Place in a clean tea towel and rub vigorously to loosen the skins. Discard the skins. Cool, then process in a food processor until finely ground.
2 Place the butter in a small pan and melt over medium heat, then cook for 3–4 minutes, or until it turns a deep golden colour. Strain any dark solids and set aside to cool (the colour will become deeper on standing).
3 Lightly whisk the egg whites in a bowl until frothy but not firm. Sift the flour, cocoa powder and icing sugar into a large bowl and stir in the ground hazelnuts. Make a well in the centre and add the egg whites and butter and mix until combined.
4 Spoon the mixture into the friand holes until three-quarters filled. Bake for 20–25 minutes, or until a skewer inserted into the centre comes out clean. Leave in the tin for a few minutes, then cool on a wire rack. Dust with icing sugar, to serve.

NUTRITION PER FRIAND
Protein 5.5 g; Fat 25 g; Carbohydrate 30 g; Dietary Fibre 2.5 g; Cholesterol 40 mg; 1475 kJ (355 cal)

COOK'S FILE

Storage time: Will keep for up to 4 days in an airtight container.

Put the hazelnuts in a tea towel and rub vigorously to loosen the skins.

Cook the butter until it turns a deep golden colour and strain any dark solids.

Spoon the mixture into the greased holes until three-quarters filled.

BLUEBERRY MUFFINS

Preparation time: 20 minutes
Total cooking time: 20 minutes
Makes 12

3 cups (375 g/12 oz) plain flour
1 tablespoon baking powder
3/4 cup (165 g/5½ oz) soft
    brown sugar
125 g (4 oz) butter, melted

2 eggs, lightly beaten
1 cup (250 ml/8 fl oz) milk
1⅓ cups (185 g/6 oz) fresh or
    thawed frozen blueberries

1 Preheat the oven to hot 210°C (415°F/Gas 6–7). Grease or brush two trays of six ½-cup (125 ml/4 fl oz) muffin holes with melted butter or oil. Sift the flour and baking powder into a large bowl. Stir in the sugar and make a well in the centre.

2 Add the combined melted butter, eggs and milk all at once, and fold until just combined. (Do not overmix, the batter should look quite lumpy.)
3 Fold in the blueberries. Spoon the batter into the prepared tin. Bake for 20 minutes, or until golden brown. Cool on a wire rack.

NUTRITION PER MUFFIN
Protein 7 g; Fat 12 g; Carbohydrate 40 g; Dietary Fibre 1.5 g; Cholesterol 65 mg; 1240 kJ (300 cal)

Make a well in the flour mixture and fold in the combined butter, eggs and milk.

Fold the blueberries into the mixture very lightly but thoroughly.

Spoon the batter into the greased muffin holes and bake until golden brown.

BREAD AND BUTTER CAKE

Preparation time: 30 minutes +
  25 minutes standing
Total cooking time: 1 hour 50 minutes
Serves 6

1/2 cup (60 g/2 oz) sultanas
2 tablespoons brandy
20 thick slices (900 g/1 lb 13 oz)
  panettone or white Hi-top
  bread
50 g (1 3/4 oz) butter, softened
1/2 cup (125 g/4 oz) caster sugar
12 eggs, lightly beaten
1 vanilla bean, cut in half, seeds
  removed and reserved

1 teaspoon grated orange rind
2 1/2 cups (600 ml/20 fl oz) cream
1 2/3 cups (410 ml/13 fl oz) milk
410 g (13 oz) can pie apple
icing sugar, to dust

1 Put the sultanas and brandy in a bowl and leave for 15 minutes. Lightly toast the panettone, then butter on one side. Preheat the oven to moderate 180°C (350°F/Gas 4). Grease and line a deep 25 cm (10 inch) round cake tin.
2 Whisk together the sugar, eggs, vanilla seeds and orange rind. Stir in the cream and milk.
3 Dip each slice of toast in the custard mixture, then arrange in an overlapping spiral pattern, working from the outside of the tin into the centre. Spoon the apple between the bread slices and add the sultanas and brandy. Gently press the top of the bread down to pack tightly.
4 Pour the custard mixture over the bread and leave for 10 minutes. Bake for 1 hour 30 minutes–1 hour 50 minutes, covering with foil after 30 minutes, until the custard is set. Cool in the tin before removing. Dust with icing sugar before serving.

NUTRITION PER SERVE
Protein 25 g; Fat 65 g; Carbohydrate 80 g; Dietary Fibre 3.5 g; Cholesterol 525 mg; 4130 kJ (987 cal)

COOK'S FILE

Note: The leftover vanilla pod can be infused in milk to flavour custards.

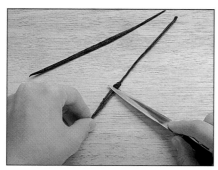

Cut the vanilla bean in half lengthways and scrape out the seeds with a small knife.

Arrange the panettone in an overlapping spiral working inwards.

Pour the custard mixture over the bread and leave for 10 minutes.

PASSIONFRUIT MOUSSE

Preparation time: 25 minutes +
  2 hours refrigeration
Total cooking time: 12 minutes
Serves 8

5–6 passionfruit
6 eggs, separated
3/4 cup (185 g/6 oz) caster sugar
1/2 teaspoon finely grated
  lemon rind
3 tablespoons lemon juice
1 tablespoon gelatine
1 1/4 cups (315 ml/10 fl oz)
  cream, lightly whipped
3/4 cup (40 g/1 1/4 oz) flaked or
  shredded coconut, toasted

1 Cut the passionfruit in half and scoop out the pulp. Strain, then measure out 3 tablespoons of juice and set aside. Add the seeds and pulp to the remaining juice and set aside. Put the egg yolks, 1/2 cup (125 g/4 oz) of the sugar, lemon rind, lemon juice and strained passionfruit juice in a heatproof bowl. Place the bowl over a pan of simmering water and, using electric beaters, beat for 10 minutes, or until thick and creamy. Remove from the heat and transfer to a glass bowl.
2 Sprinkle the gelatine over 1/2 cup (125 ml/4 fl oz) water in a small bowl and leave until spongy. Place the bowl in a pan of just boiled water (the water should come half way up the bowl) and stir until dissolved. Add the gelatine to

the mousse mixture and mix well. Mix in the passionfruit pulp and leave until cold, then gently fold in the whipped cream.
3 Using electric beaters, whisk the egg whites until soft peaks form and gradually whisk in the remaining sugar, beating until the sugar has dissolved. Fold the egg whites into the mousse mixture quickly and lightly. Spoon into eight 1-cup (250 ml/8 fl oz) ramekins or elegant stemmed wine glasses, and refrigerate for 2 hours, or until set. Sprinkle with the coconut just before serving.

NUTRITION PER SERVE
Protein 7 g; Fat 22 g; Carbohydrate 25 g; Dietary Fibre 2.5 g; Cholesterol 185 mg; 1350 kJ (325 cal)

Scoop the pulp out of the passionfruit and strain.

Beat the mixture over a pan of simmering water until thick and creamy.

Lightly fold the whisked egg whites into the mousse mixture.

PASSIONFRUIT MELTING MOMENTS

Preparation time: 40 minutes
Total cooking time: 20 minutes
Makes 14 filled biscuits

250 g (8 oz) unsalted butter
1/3 cup (40 g/1 1/4 oz) icing sugar
1 teaspoon vanilla essence
1 1/2 cups (185 g/6 oz) self-
  raising flour
1/2 cup (60 g/2 oz) custard
  powder

Passionfruit Filling
60 g (2 oz) butter
1/2 cup (60 g/2 oz) icing sugar
1 1/2 tablespoons passionfruit pulp

1 Preheat the oven to moderate 180°C (350°F/Gas 4). Line two baking trays with baking paper. Beat the butter and sugar until light and creamy. Beat in the vanilla essence. Sift in the flour and custard powder and mix to a soft dough. Roll level tablespoons of the mixture into 28 balls and place on the trays. Flatten slightly with a floured fork.
2 Bake for 20 minutes, or until lightly golden. Cool on a wire rack.
3 To make the filling, beat the butter and sugar until light and creamy, then beat in the passionfruit pulp. Use the filling to sandwich the biscuits together. Leave to firm before serving.

NUTRITION PER BISCUIT
Protein 1.5 g; Fat 20 g; Carbohydrate 17 g; Dietary Fibre 1 g; Cholesterol 55 mg; 995 kJ (235 cal)

COOK'S FILE

Storage time: The biscuits will keep for up to 4 days in an airtight container.

Variation: You can vary the flavour of the filling. To make a coffee filling, for example, dissolve 2 teaspoons of instant coffee in 2 teaspoons water and add to the butter and sugar mixture. Beat until well combined.

Beat the butter and sugar together until creamy, then add the vanilla essence.

Roll the mixture into balls, put them on the baking trays and flatten with a fork.

Beat together the butter and icing sugar, then add the passionfruit pulp.

CHOCOLATE BROWNIES

Preparation time: 20 minutes +
  2 hours refrigeration
Total cooking time: 55 minutes
Makes 24

$^1/_3$ cup (40 g/1$^1/_4$ oz) plain flour
$^1/_2$ cup (60 g/2 oz) cocoa powder
2 cups (500 g/1 lb) sugar
1 cup (125 g/4 oz) chopped
  pecans or golden walnuts
250 g (8 oz) dark chocolate
250 g (8 oz) butter
2 teaspoons vanilla essence
4 eggs, lightly beaten

1 Preheat the oven to moderate 180°C (350°F/Gas 4). Brush a 20 x 30 cm (8 x 12 inch) cake tin with melted butter or oil. Line the base with baking paper, extending over the two long sides.
2 Sift the flour and cocoa into a bowl and add the sugar and nuts. Mix together and make a well in the centre.
3 Using a large sharp knife, chop the chocolate into small pieces and add to the dry ingredients.
4 Melt the butter in a small pan over low heat and add to the dry ingredients with the vanilla and eggs. Mix well.
5 Pour into the tin, smooth the surface and bake for 50 minutes (the mixture will still be a bit soft on the inside). Refrigerate for at least 2 hours before cutting and serving.

NUTRITION PER BROWNIE
Protein 6 g; Fat 20 g; Carbohydrate 30 g; Dietary Fibre 0.5 g; Cholesterol 145 mg; 1265 kJ (300 cal)

COOK'S FILE

Note: Use a good-quality chocolate. Cooking chocolate is not suitable for this recipe.

Add the sugar and chopped nuts to the flour and cocoa.

Use a sharp knife to chop the chocolate into small pieces.

Melt the butter and add to the chocolate and nut mixture with the vanilla and eggs.

PORTUGUESE CUSTARD TARTS

Preparation time: 40 minutes
Total cooking time: 40 minutes
Makes 12

1¼ cups (155 g/5 oz) plain flour
25 g (¾ oz) vegetable shortening, chopped and softened
30 g (1 oz) butter, chopped and softened
1 cup (250 g/8 oz) sugar
2 cups (500 ml/16 fl oz) milk
3 tablespoons cornflour
1 tablespoon custard powder
4 egg yolks
1 teaspoon vanilla essence

1 Sift the flour into a large bowl and add about ¾ cup (185 ml/6 fl oz) water, or enough to form a soft dough. Gather the dough into a ball, then roll out on non-stick baking paper to form a 24 x 30 cm (9½ x 12 inch) rectangle. Spread the vegetable shortening over the surface. Roll up from the short edge to form a log.

2 Roll the dough out into a rectangle again, and spread with the butter. Roll up again into a roll and slice into 12 even pieces. Working from the centre outwards, use your fingertips to press each round out to a circle that is large enough to cover the base and sides of twelve ⅓-cup (80 ml/2¾ fl oz) muffin holes. Press into the tin and refrigerate while preparing the filling.

3 Put the sugar and ⅓ cup (80 ml/2¾ fl oz) of water into a pan, and stir over low heat until the sugar dissolves.
4 Mix a little milk with the cornflour and custard powder to form a smooth paste, and add to the pan with the remaining milk, egg yolks and vanilla. Stir over low heat until the mixture thickens. Put in a bowl, cover and cool.
5 Preheat the oven to hot 220°C (425°F/Gas 7). Divide the filling among the pastry bases and bake for 25–30 minutes, or until the custard is set and the tops have browned. Cool in the tins, then transfer to a wire rack.

NUTRITION PER TART
Protein 3.5 g; Fat 7 g; Carbohydrate 35 g; Dietary Fibre 0.5 g; Cholesterol 75 mg; 892 kJ (215 cal)

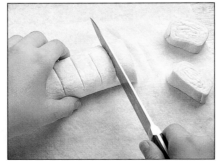

Roll out the dough and spread with the vegetable shortening.

Slice the roll of dough into 12 even pieces with a sharp knife.

With your fingertips press each round out to a circle and press into the tin.

GOURMET CARROT CAKE

Preparation time: 40 minutes
Total cooking time: 1 hour 30 minutes
Serves 12

1 cup (125 g/4 oz) self-raising
   flour
1 cup (125 g/4 oz) plain flour
2 teaspoons ground cinnamon
1/2 teaspoon ground cloves
1 teaspoon ground ginger
1/2 teaspoon ground nutmeg
1 teaspoon bicarbonate of soda
1 cup (250 ml/8 fl oz) oil
1 cup (185 g/6 oz) soft brown
   sugar
1/2 cup (125 ml/4 fl oz) golden
   syrup

4 eggs
2 1/2 cups (390 g/12 1/2 oz) grated
   carrot
1/2 cup (60 g/2 oz) chopped
   walnuts or pecans
175 g (6 oz) cream cheese,
   softened
60 g (2 oz) butter, softened
1 1/2 cups (185 g/6 oz) icing
   sugar
1 teaspoon vanilla essence
1–2 teaspoons lemon juice

1 Preheat the oven to warm 160°C (315°F/Gas 2–3). Brush a deep 23 cm (9 inch) round cake tin with melted butter or oil. Line the base and side with baking paper. Sift the flours, spices and soda into a large bowl and make a well in the centre.

2 Whisk together the oil, sugar, syrup and eggs and gradually stir into the the dry ingredients until smooth. Stir in the carrot and walnuts. Spoon the mixture into the tin. Bake for 1 1/2 hours, or until a skewer comes out clean when inserted into the centre. Cool in the tin, then on a wire rack.

3 Beat the cream cheese and butter until smooth. Gradually add the icing sugar alternately with the vanilla and lemon juice, beating until light and creamy. Spread the icing over the cake (or cut the cake in half horizontally, sandwich the layers together with half the icing and spread the rest on top).

NUTRITION PER SERVE
Protein 6.5 g; Fat 35 g; Carbohydrate 60 g; Dietary Fibre 2 g; Cholesterol 85 mg; 2330 kJ (555 cal)

In a large bowl, whisk together the oil, sugar, syrup and eggs.

Add the carrot and walnuts and mix together until smooth.

The cake is cooked if a skewer comes out clean when inserted in the centre.

CHOCOLATE MUD CAKE

Preparation time: 25 minutes
Total cooking time: 1 hour 45 minutes
Serves 12

1 cup (125 g/4 oz) plain flour
1 cup (125 g/4 oz) self-raising
 flour
1/2 cup (60 g/2 oz) dark cocoa
 powder
1/2 teaspoon bicarbonate of soda
21/2 cups (625 g/1 lb 4 oz) sugar
450 g (14 oz) dark chocolate,
 chopped
450 g (14 oz) butter
1/2 cup (125 ml/4 fl oz)
 buttermilk
2 tablespoons oil
2 tablespoons instant espresso
 coffee granules or powder
4 eggs

1 Preheat the oven to warm 160°C (315°F/Gas 2–3). Brush a deep, 23 cm (9 inch) square cake tin with melted butter or oil. Line the base and sides with baking paper, extending at least 2 cm (3/4 inch) above the rim.
2 Sift the flours, cocoa and soda into a large bowl. Stir in the sugar and make a well in the centre.
3 Put 250 g (8 oz) of the chocolate and 250 g (8 oz) of the butter in a pan. Add 3/4 cup (185 ml/6 fl oz) of water and stir over low heat until the butter and chocolate dissolve. Using a large metal spoon, gradually stir the chocolate mixture into the dry ingredients.
4 Whisk together the buttermilk, oil, coffee and eggs in a large jug and add to the cake mixture. Stir until the ingredients are well combined and smooth. Pour the mixture into the tin

and bake for 1 hour 40 minutes, or until a skewer comes out clean when inserted in the centre. Leave the cake in the tin to cool completely before turning out.
5 Combine the remaining chocolate and butter in a small pan and stir over low heat until smooth. Cool to room temperature, stirring often, until the mixture is thick enough to spread.

(You can hasten this process by refrigerating the mixture.) Turn the cake upside down so that the uneven top becomes the base, and spread the icing completely over the cake. Allow the icing to set slightly before serving.

NUTRITION PER SERVE
Protein 8 g; Fat 45 g; Carbohydrate 95 g; Dietary Fibre 1.5 g; Cholesterol 157 mg; 3385 kJ (810 cal)

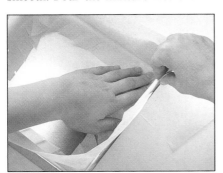

Line the base and sides of the tin with baking paper, extending well over the rim.

Gradually stir the chocolate mixture into the dry ingredients.

Pour in the buttermilk mixture and stir until well combined.

PEAR AND ALMOND FLAN

Preparation time: 15 minutes +
  2 hours 30 minutes chilling
Total cooking time: 1 hour 10 minutes
Serves 8

1¼ cups (155 g/5 oz) plain flour
90 g (3 oz) chilled butter, chopped
¼ cup (60 g/2 oz) caster sugar
2 egg yolks

Filling
165 g (5½ oz) butter, softened
²/3 cup (160 g/5½ oz) caster sugar
3 eggs
1¼ cups (230 g/7½ oz) almond
  meal
1½ tablespoons plain flour
2 ripe pears

1 Grease a shallow 24 cm (9½ inch) round flan tin with a removable base. Place the flour, butter and sugar in a food processor and process until the mixture resembles breadcrumbs. Add the egg yolks and about 1 tablespoon of water until mixture just comes together. Turn out onto a lightly floured surface and gather into a ball. Wrap in plastic wrap and refrigerate for 30 minutes. Preheat the oven to moderate 180°C (350°F/Gas 4).
2 Roll the pastry between baking paper dusted with flour until large enough to line the tin. Remove the baking paper, lift the pastry into the tin, and trim off any excess. Sparsely prick the bottom with a fork. Line with baking paper, fill with baking beads and bake for 10 minutes. Remove the beads and bake for 10 minutes.

3 To make the filling, mix the butter and sugar with electric beaters for 30 seconds (don't cream the mixture). Add the eggs one at a time, beating after each addition. Fold in the almond meal and flour and spread the filling smoothly over the cooled pastry base.
4 Peel and halve the pears lengthways and remove the cores. Cut the pears crossways into 3 mm (1/8 inch) slices. Separate the slices slightly, then place each half on top of the tart to form a cross. Bake for about 50 minutes, or until the filling has set (the middle may still be a little soft). Cool in the tin, then refrigerate for at least 2 hours before serving.

NUTRITION PER SERVE
Protein 7 g; Fat 30 g; Carbohydrate 48 g; Dietary Fibre 2 g; Cholesterol 165 mg; 2085 kJ (500 cal)

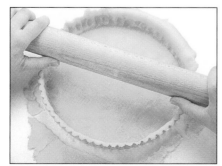

Trim off any excess pastry by rolling a rolling pin over the tin.

Fold in the almond meal and flour and mix until well combined.

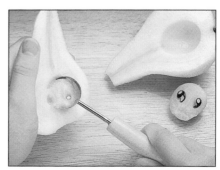

Halve each pear lengthways and carefully remove the core.

BAKED CHEESECAKE

Preparation time: 30 minutes +
  20 minutes refrigeration + chilling
Total cooking time: 55 minutes
Serves 8

250 g (8 oz) butternut cookies
1 teaspoon mixed spice
100 g (3½ oz) butter, melted
500 g (1 lb) cream cheese,
  softened
⅔ cup (160 g/5½ oz) caster
  sugar
4 eggs
1 teaspoon vanilla essence
1 tablespoon orange juice
1 tablespoon grated orange rind

Topping
1 cup (250 g/8 oz) sour cream
½ teaspoon vanilla essence
3 teaspoons orange juice
1 tablespoon caster sugar
freshly grated nutmeg

1 Lightly grease the base of a 20 cm (8 inch) springform tin. Finely crush the biscuits in a food processor for 30 seconds, or put them in a plastic bag and roll with a rolling pin. Transfer to a bowl and add the mixed spice and butter. Stir until all the crumbs are moistened, then spoon the mixture into the prepared tin and press it firmly into the base and side. Refrigerate for 20 minutes, or until firm.

2 Preheat the oven to moderate 180°C (350°F/Gas 4). Beat the cream cheese until smooth. Add the sugar and beat until smooth. Add the eggs, one at a time, beating well after each addition. Mix in the vanilla, orange juice and orange rind.

3 Pour the mixture into the crumb case and bake for 45 minutes, or until just firm. To make the topping, combine the sour cream, vanilla, orange juice and sugar in a bowl. Spread over the hot cheesecake, sprinkle with nutmeg and return to the oven for 7 minutes. Cool, then refrigerate until firm.

NUTRITION PER SERVE
Protein 10 g; Fat 50 g; Carbohydrate 45 g; Dietary Fibre 0.5 g; Cholesterol 230 mg; 2885 kJ (690 cal)

Press the biscuit mixture into a springform tin with the back of a spoon.

Add the eggs one at a time to the cream cheese mixture and beat well.

When the filling is smooth, mix in the vanilla, orange juice and rind.

TIRAMISU

Preparation time: 30 minutes +
2 hours refrigeration
Total cooking time: Nil
Serves 6

3 cups (750 ml/24 fl oz) strong
black coffee, cooled
3 tablespoons Marsala or
coffee-flavoured liqueur
2 eggs, separated
3 tablespoons caster sugar
250 g (8 oz) mascarpone
1 cup (250 ml/8 fl oz) cream,
whipped

16 large sponge fingers
2 tablespoons dark cocoa
powder

1 Mix together the coffee and Marsala in a bowl and set aside. Using electric beaters, beat the egg yolks and sugar in a bowl for 3 minutes, or until thick and pale. Add the mascarpone and mix until just combined. Transfer to a large bowl and fold in the cream.
2 Beat the egg whites until soft peaks form. Fold quickly and lightly into the cream mixture.
3 Dip half the biscuits into the coffee mixture, then drain off any excess coffee and arrange in the base of a 2.5 litre ceramic dish. Spread half the cream mixture over the biscuits.
4 Dip the remaining biscuits into the remaining coffee mixture and repeat the layers. Smooth the surface and dust liberally with the cocoa powder. Refrigerate for at least 2 hours, or until firm.

NUTRITION PER SERVE
Protein 7.5 g; Fat 24 g; Carbohydrate 28 g; Dietary Fibre 1 g; Cholesterol 180 mg; 1545 kJ (370 cal)

COOK'S FILE

Storage time: Tiramisu is best made a day ahead to let the flavours develop. Refrigerate until ready to serve.

Add the mascarpone to the egg yolks and sugar and mix well.

Fold the beaten egg whites gently into the cream mixture.

Dip half the biscuits in the coffee mixture, drain, and arrange in the serving dish.

FLORENTINES

Preparation time: 15 minutes
Total cooking time: 15 minutes
Makes 12

55 g (2 oz) butter
1/4 cup (45 g/11/2 oz) soft
   brown sugar
2 teaspoons honey
1/4 cup (25 g/3/4 oz) flaked
   almonds, roughly chopped
2 tablespoons chopped dried
   apricots
2 tablespoons chopped glacé
   cherries
2 tablespoons mixed peel

1/3 cup (40 g/11/4 oz) plain flour,
   sifted
120 g (4 oz) dark chocolate

1 Preheat the oven to moderate 180°C (350°F/Gas 4). Melt the butter, brown sugar and honey in a pan until the butter is melted and all the ingredients are combined. Remove from the heat and add the almonds, apricots, glacé cherries, mixed peel and the flour. Mix well.

2 Grease and line two baking trays with baking paper. Place level tablespoons of the mixture well apart on the trays. Reshape and flatten the biscuits into 5 cm (2 inch) rounds before cooking.

3 Bake for 10 minutes, or until lightly browned. Cool on the tray, then allow to cool completely on a wire rack.

4 To melt the chocolate, break it up into small pieces and put it in a heatproof bowl. Bring a pan of water to a simmer, remove from the heat and place the bowl over the pan. Stir the chocolate until melted. Spread the melted chocolate on the bottom of each florentine and, using a fork, make a wavy pattern on the chocolate before it sets. Let the chocolate set before serving.

NUTRITION PER BISCUIT
Protein 1.5 g; Fat 8 g; Carbohydrate 15 g; Dietary Fibre 1 g; Cholesterol 12 mg; 550 kJ (130 cal)

Add the almonds, apricots, glacé cherries, mixed peel and flour to the pan.

Flatten the mixture with the back of a teaspoon and reshape into rounds.

Use a fork to make a wavy pattern in the melted chocolate before it sets.

MACADAMIA AND WHITE CHOCOLATE COOKIES

Preparation time: 15 minutes +
30 minutes refrigeration
Total cooking time: 20 minutes
Makes about 25

1¹/₃ cups (180 g/6 oz)
  macadamia nuts
1 egg
³/₄ cup (140 g/4¹/₂ oz) soft
  brown sugar
2 tablespoons white sugar
1 teaspoon vanilla essence
¹/₂ cup (125 ml/4 fl oz) oil
¹/₂ cup (60 g/2 oz) plain flour
¹/₄ cup (30 g/1 oz) self-raising
  flour
¹/₄ teaspoon cinnamon
¹/₂ cup (30 g/1 oz) shredded
  coconut
³/₄ cup (130 g/4¹/₂ oz) white
  chocolate bits

1 Put the nuts on a baking tray and bake for 5 minutes, or until lightly toasted. Cool and roughly chop.
2 Using electric beaters, beat the egg and sugars in a bowl until light and fluffy. Add the vanilla and oil. Using a wooden spoon, stir in the sifted flours, cinnamon, coconut, macadamias and chocolate, and mix well. Refrigerate for 30 minutes.

Preheat the oven to moderate 180°C (350°F/Gas 4). Grease and line two baking trays.
3 Form rounded tablespoons of the mixture into balls and place on the baking trays, pressing the mixture together with your fingertips if crumbly. Bake for 12–15 minutes, or until golden. Cool slightly on the trays, then transfer to a wire rack.

NUTRITION PER COOKIE
Protein 1.5 g; Fat 10 g; Carbohydrate 13 g; Dietary Fibre 0.5 g; Cholesterol 8 mg; 695 kJ (165 cal)

COOK'S FILE

Variation: Dark chocolate bits can be used instead of white chocolate.

Roughly chop the macadamias into small pieces with a large sharp knife.

Stir in the flours, cinnamon, coconut, macadamias and chocolate and mix well.

Form the mixture into balls, pressing it together firmly.

STICKY DATE PUDDINGS

Preparation time: 30 minutes
Total cooking time: 50 minutes
Serves 6

180 g (6 oz) dates, pitted and
    roughly chopped
1 teaspoon bicarbonate of soda
75 g (2¹/₂ oz) butter, softened
²/₃ cup (155 g/5 oz) firmly
    packed soft brown sugar
1 teaspoon vanilla essence
2 eggs
1¹/₂ cups (185 g/6 oz) self-
    raising flour, sifted
1 cup (100 g/3¹/₂ oz) walnut
    halves, roughly chopped

Caramel Sauce
²/₃ cup (155 g/5 oz) firmly
    packed soft brown sugar
60 g (2 oz) butter
1 cup (250 ml/8 fl oz) cream

1 Preheat the oven to moderate 180°C (350°F/Gas 4). Lightly brush six 1-cup (250 ml/8 fl oz) moulds with melted butter and line the bases with circles of baking paper. Put the dates and soda in a pan and pour in 1 cup (250 ml/8 fl oz) of water. Bring to the boil, remove from the heat and set aside to cool (the mixture will become foamy).

2 Beat the softened butter, sugar and vanilla with electric beaters until light and creamy. Add one egg, beat well and fold through 1 tablespoon of the flour. Add the other egg and repeat the process.

3 Fold through the remaining flour, walnuts and date mixture along with all the liquid, and mix well. Divide the mixture among the moulds, filling

them three-quarters full. Bake for 30–35 minutes, or until slightly risen and firm to the touch.

4 To make the sauce, put the brown sugar, butter and cream in a pan and simmer for 5 minutes. When the puddings are cooked, remove from the oven and prick a few holes in each one. Drizzle with some of the caramel sauce and return to the oven for

5 minutes to allow the sauce to sink in. Loosen the side of each pudding with a small spatula or flexible knife. Carefully turn out, remove the baking paper and serve with the remaining caramel sauce.

NUTRITION PER PUDDING
Protein 9 g; Fat 50 g; Carbohydrate 95 g; Dietary Fibre 5 g; Cholesterol 175 mg; 3523 kJ (840 cal)

Combine the dates, soda and water in a small pan and bring to the boil.

Fold through the remaining flour, walnuts and date mixture.

To make the syrup, combine the sugar, butter and cream in a pan and simmer.

PECAN AND COFFEE BISCOTTI

Preparation time: 20 minutes +
  20 minutes cooling
Total cooking time: 1 hour 5 minutes
Makes 40

1³/4 cups (215 g/7 oz) plain flour
1/2 teaspoon baking powder
2/3 cup (160 g/5¹/2 oz) caster
  sugar
60 g (2 oz) butter
2 eggs
1/2 teaspoon vanilla essence
2 tablespoons instant coffee
  granules
1¹/3 cups (135 g/4 oz) whole
  pecans
1/2 teaspoon caster sugar, extra

1 Preheat the oven to moderate 180°C (350°F/Gas 4) and line two baking trays with baking paper. Place the sifted flour, baking powder, sugar and a pinch of salt in a food processor and mix for 1–2 seconds. Add the butter and mix until the mixture resembles fine breadcrumbs. Add the eggs and vanilla and process until the mixture is smooth.
2 Transfer the dough to a well-floured surface and knead in the coffee and pecans. Divide into two equal portions and, using lightly floured hands, shape each into a log about 20 cm (8 inches) long. Place the logs on the baking trays and sprinkle with the extra sugar. Press the top of each log down gently to make an oval.
3 Bake for about 35 minutes, or until golden. Remove and set aside to cool for about 20 minutes. Reduce the oven temperature to warm 170°C (325°F/Gas 3).

4 Cut the logs into 1 cm (1/2 inch) slices. Turn the baking paper over, then spread the biscotti well apart on the tray so that they do not touch. Return to the oven and bake for a further 30 minutes, or until they just begin to colour. Cool completely before storing in an airtight container.

NUTRITION PER SERVE
Protein 1.5 g; Fat 4.5 g; Carbohydrate 8 g; Dietary Fibre 0.5 g; Cholesterol 13 mg; 325 kJ (78 cal)

COOK'S FILE

Hint: Cook in the top half of the oven, and move lower halfway through cooking.

Add the eggs and vanilla and process until the mixture is smooth.

On a well-floured surface, knead the coffee and pecans into the dough.

When the logs are cool enough to handle, cut into slices.

Dessert Sauces

Ice cream, pancakes, fresh fruit, waffles and puddings can all be elevated from the ordinary to the sublime in minutes with these mouth-watering sauces. From traditional favourites to exciting new flavour combinations, you'll be surprised how quickly the dessert bowls are scraped clean.

COFFEE SAUCE

Whisk 3 egg yolks, 2 tablespoons soft brown sugar and $1/2$ teaspoon cornflour until thick and pale in colour. Heat $2/3$ cup (170 ml/$5^1/2$ fl oz) milk and 2 tablespoons ground coffee in a pan until almost boiling. Strain through a fine sieve. Gradually whisk into the egg mixture. Return the mixture to the pan and stir over low heat until it thickens and coats the back of a wooden spoon. Remove from the heat and allow the mixture to cool. Stir through $1/4$ cup (60 ml/2 fl oz) lightly whipped cream. For best results, serve the coffee sauce on the day it is made. Makes 2 cups (500 ml/16 fl oz).

CHOCOLATE FUDGE SAUCE

Roughly chop 250 g (8 oz) dark chocolate. Place in a pan with $3/4$ cup (185 ml/6 fl oz) cream, 50 g ($1^3/4$ oz) butter and 1 tablespoon golden syrup. Stir over low heat until the mixture is smooth and combined. Add a little more cream if the sauce is slightly grainy. Serve hot over ice cream, waffles, pancakes, poached fruit or puddings. Refrigerate in a sealed container for up to 1 month and gently reheat to serve. Makes 2 cups (500 ml/16 fl oz).
Variation: Add 2 tablespoons coffee or chocolate liqueur, such as Kahlua or Baileys, to the sauce before serving.

BRANDY BUTTER

In a food processor, process 125 g (4 oz) softened unsalted butter and $1/2$ cup (60 g/2 oz) icing sugar until softened and combined. Gradually add $1/4$ cup (60 ml/2 fl oz) brandy, beating well after each addition (do not overbeat the butter or it will curdle). Brandy butter is traditionally served with Christmas pudding. If you wish to shape the brandy butter, line a baking tray with foil, spread with the brandy butter, cover and refrigerate until firm. Once the butter is firm, use biscuit cutters to cut out shapes to serve. Brandy butter will keep refrigerated for up to 1 month. Makes 2 cups (500 ml/16 fl oz).

BUTTERSCOTCH SAUCE

Place 125 g (4 oz) butter and ¹/2 cup (95 g/3 oz) soft brown sugar in a pan and stir over low heat until the sugar has dissolved. Bring to the boil and add 2 tablespoons golden syrup and ¹/2 cup (125 ml/4 fl oz) cream. Reduce the heat and simmer for 10 minutes, or until slightly thickened. Remove from the heat and add 1 teaspoon vanilla essence. Serve either hot or cold. Makes 1¹/2 cups (375 ml/12 fl oz).

RASPBERRY SAUCE

In a small pan, stir to dissolve ¹/2 cup (125 g/4 oz) sugar in ¹/2 cup (125 ml/4 oz) water over low heat. Bring to the boil and cook for 10 minutes or until reduced and slightly thickened. Set aside to cool. In a food processor or blender, purée 300 g (10 oz) fresh or thawed frozen raspberries, the sugar syrup and 1 tablespoon lemon juice. Strain in a fine sieve to remove any seeds. This sauce can also be kept in a bottle or airtight container in the fridge for up to 1 week. Makes about 1¹/2 cups (375 ml/12 fl oz).

From left to right: Blueberry and star anise sauce; Coffee sauce; Chocolate chilli sauce; Butterscotch sauce; Brandy butter; Raspberry sauce; Chocolate fudge sauce.

Variation: This recipe can also be made with strawberries, blueberries, blackberries or a combination of your favourite berries. Serve with ice creams, sorbets, yoghurt, fresh or poached fruit, pies or tarts.

CHOCOLATE CHILLI SAUCE

Combine 1²/3 cups (250 g/8 oz) roughly chopped dark chocolate (not cooking chocolate), 1 cup (250 ml/8 fl oz) cream, 30 g (1 oz) butter and 1 teaspoon chilli powder in a pan. Cook over very low heat until all the chocolate is melted and the mixture is smooth. This sauce can be refrigerated for up to 2 weeks and gently reheated when required. Serve either warm or cold with fresh fruit such as strawberries and raspberries; with profiteroles, ice cream, cassata, waffles or as a sauce with a slice of cake. Makes about 2 cups (500 ml/16 fl oz).

BLUEBERRY AND STAR ANISE SAUCE

In a small pan heat ¹/2 cup (125 ml/4 fl oz) water and add ¹/4 cup (60 g/2 oz) caster sugar and stir until dissolved. Reduce the heat, add 2 star anise and simmer for 8–10 minutes, or until the mixture begins to thicken. Add 300 g (10 oz) fresh blueberries and cook for a further 8–10 minutes, or until the blueberries begin to break up. Remove from the heat and allow to cool. Remove the star anise. Purée the mixture in a food processor or blender until smooth. Serve either hot or cold. This sauce can be bottled and kept in the refrigerator for up to 1 week. Makes about 1¹/2 cups (375 ml/12 fl oz).

Variation: If you want a stronger aniseed flavour, add 1 teaspoon of Pernod or Sambuca to the sauce before you purée it. Frozen blueberries may be used for this recipe, though they will give off a little more juice.

MIXED NUT TARTLETS

Preparation time: 45 minutes +
  30 minutes refrigeration
Total cooking time: 50 minutes
Makes 10

300 g (10 oz) mixed nuts
  (pecans, macadamias or
  hazelnuts)
3 cups (375 g/12 oz) plain flour
230 g (7½ oz) butter, chopped
3 tablespoons soft brown sugar
2 tablespoons white sugar
3 tablespoons light corn syrup
30 g (1 oz) butter, melted
2 eggs, lightly beaten

1 Preheat the oven to moderate 180°C (350°F/Gas 4). Spread the nuts on a baking tray and bake for 7 minutes. Set aside.

2 Place the sifted flour and butter in a food processor. Pulse for 10 seconds, or until the mixture resembles fine breadcrumbs. Add about 1/3 cup (80 ml/2¾ fl oz) water and process until the mixture just comes together. Add another tablespoon of water if needed. Turn out onto a lightly floured surface and gather into a ball. Refrigerate for 20 minutes.

3 Divide the pastry into 10 portions. Roll each portion out on a lightly floured surface and line 10 fluted, 8 cm (3 inch) flan tins. Trim any excess pastry, then refrigerate for 10 minutes. Put the tins on two baking trays. Cut sheets of crumpled baking paper to line the base and side of each tin. Place baking beads or rice in the tins and bake for 10 minutes. Remove the beads and paper and bake for 10–15 minutes.

4 Divide the nuts among the pastry shells. Whisk together the remaining ingredients and drizzle the mixture over the nuts. Bake for 15–20 minutes, or until just set and golden. Allow to cool completely before serving.

NUTRITION PER TARTLET
Protein 10 g; Fat 40 g; Carbohydrate 40 g; Dietary Fibre 3.5 g; Cholesterol 305 mg; 2312 kJ (550 cal)

Add the water and process until the mixture just comes together.

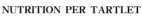

Remove the baking paper and beads and bake for a further 10–15 minutes.

Whisk together the ingredients for the syrup and pour over the nuts.

BAKLAVA

Preparation time: 25 minutes +
   overnight refrigeration
Total cooking time: 50 minutes
Serves 10

Syrup
2 cups (500 g/1 lb) sugar
2 whole cloves
1 slice lemon
1/2 teaspoon ground cardamom

1 1/2 cups (235 g/7 1/2 oz) finely
   chopped unblanched almonds
1 1/2 cups (185 g/6 oz) finely
   chopped walnuts
1 teaspoon ground cardamom
1 teaspoon mixed spice

1/2 cup (125 g/4 oz) caster sugar
16 sheets filo pastry
2/3 cup (160 g/5 1/2 oz) unsalted
   butter, melted

1 To make the syrup, put the sugar, cloves, lemon, cardamom and 2 cups (500 ml/16 fl oz) of water in a large heavy-based pan and bring to the boil, stirring. Simmer for 12 minutes, remove the cloves and lemon and refrigerate.

2 Preheat the oven to moderate 180°C (350°F/Gas 4). Grease an 18 x 28 cm (7 x 11 inch) shallow tin. Mix the almonds, walnuts, cardamom, mixed spice and sugar in a bowl. Take 4 sheets of filo and, layering the pastry, brush each sheet lightly with some of the melted butter. Fold the sheets in half crossways, trim the edges so the pastry fits the base of the tin, then put in the tin.

3 Sprinkle one third of the nut mixture over the filo, then top with another 4 sheets of filo, brushing each with some of the melted butter and then layering, folding and trimming.

4 Repeat the layers twice more. Trim the edges of the top layers of filo, brush with melted butter and score into large diamonds. Bake for 30–35 minutes, or until golden brown and crisp.

5 Pour the cold syrup over the hot baklava and refrigerate overnight before cutting into diamonds.

NUTRITION PER SERVE
Protein 9 g; Fat 40 g; Carbohydrate 75 g; Dietary Fibre 3.5 g; Cholesterol 40 mg; 2835 kJ (675 cal)

Brush each sheet of pastry with melted butter and fold in half crossways.

Sprinkle some of the nut mixture over the the pastry.

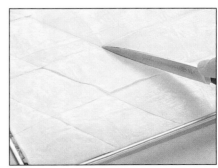

Use a sharp knife to score the top layers into diamonds.

TIPSY STRAWBERRY TRIFLE

Preparation time: 20 minutes +
  4 hours refrigeration
Total cooking time: Nil
Serves 8

2 x 85 g (3 oz) packets red jelly
  crystals
1 cup (250 ml/8 fl oz) brandy
  or rum
1 cup (250 ml/8 fl oz) milk
2 x 250 g (8 oz) packets thin
  sponge finger biscuits
2 x 250 g (8 oz) punnets
  strawberries, hulled and
  sliced
3 cups (750 ml/24 fl oz)
  ready-made custard
1¼ cups (315 ml/10 fl oz)
  cream, whipped

1 Mix the jelly crystals with 1¾ cups (440 ml/14 fl oz) of boiling water and stir to dissolve. Pour into a shallow tin and refrigerate until the jelly has just set but is not firm.
2 Combine the brandy and milk in a dish. Dip half the biscuits in the brandy mixture then place in a single layer in a 3-litre glass or ceramic dish. Spoon half the jelly over the biscuits. Scatter with half the strawberries and then half of the custard.
3 Dip the remaining sponge fingers in the brandy mixture and place evenly over the custard, followed by the remaining jelly and custard. Spread the whipped cream evenly over the custard and top with the remaining strawberries. Cover and refrigerate for 4 hours before serving.

NUTRITION PER SERVE
Protein 13 g; Fat 24 g; Carbohydrate 75 g; Dietary Fibre 2 g; Cholesterol 165 mg; 2570 kJ (615 cal)

Using a small sharp knife, hull the strawberries and cut into slices.

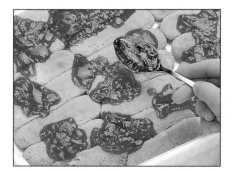

Spoon half the jelly over the biscuits before scattering on half the strawberries.

Dip the remaining biscuits in the brandy mixture and layer evenly over the custard.

INDEX

INTERNATIONAL GLOSSARY OF INGREDIENTS

capsicum	red or green pepper	fresh coriander	fresh cilantro
eggplant	aubergine	English spinach	spinach
zucchini	courgette	cream	single cream
tomato paste (Aus.)	tomato purée, double concentrate (UK)	tomato purée (Aus.)	sieved crushed tomatoes/ passata (UK)

Published by Murdoch Books®, a division of Murdoch Magazines Pty Limited, 45 Jones Street, Ultimo NSW 2007.

Managing Editor: Jane Price **Editors:** Rachel Carter, Pip Vice **Designer:** Michelle Cutler **Editorial Assistant:** Stephanie Kistner **Food Director:** Jody Vassallo **Food Editors:** Roslyn Anderson, Lulu Grimes **Recipe Development:** Roslyn Anderson, Michelle Earl, Stephanie Elias, Jo Glynn, Lulu Grimes, Kathy Knudsen, Barbara Lowery, Kerrie Mullins, Sally Parker, Justine Poole, Wendy Quisumbing, Jo Richardson, Tracy Rutherford, Jody Vassallo, Lovoni Welch **Home Economists:** Michelle Lawton, Beth Mitchell, Kerrie Mullins, Justine Poole, Margot Smithyman **Nutritionist:** Thérèse Abbey **Photographers:** Joe Filshie, Reg Morrison (steps) **Food Stylists:** Marie-Hélène Clauzon, Michelle Norianto **Food Preparation:** Kerrie Mullins. **CEO & Publisher:** Anne Wilson **International Sales Director:** Mark Newman.

The nutritional information provided for each recipe does not include any accompaniments, such as rice, unless they are listed in the ingredients. The values are approximations and can be affected by biological and seasonal variations in food, the unknown composition of some manufactured foods and uncertainty in the dietary database. Nutrient data given are derived primarily from the NUTTAB95 database produced by the Australian New Zealand Food Authority.
National Library of Australia Cataloguing-in-Publication Data. Favourite deli food to make at home. Includes index. ISBN 0 86411 870 8. 1. Delicatessens. 2. Cookery. I. Title: Family circle (Sydney, N.SW). (Series: Family circle step-by-step). 641.5. First printed 1999. Printed by Prestige Litho, Queensland. PRINTED IN AUSTRALIA.